The Clasp of Civilizations

The Clasp of Civilizations

Globalization and Religion in a Multicultural World

Richard Hartz

Nalanda International
Los Angeles (USA)

PRINTWORLD
Publishers of Indian Traditions

Cataloging in Publication Data — DK
[Courtesy: D.K. Agencies (P) Ltd. <docinfo@dkagencies.com>]

Hartz, Richard, 1951-
The clasp of civilizations : globalization and religion in a multicultural world / Richard Hartz.
p. cm.
Includes bibliographical references (p.).
ISBN 9788124608050

1. Globalization – Religious aspects. 2. Religion and culture. 3. Religion and culture – India. 4. Civilization. 5. India – Civilization. I. Title.

DDC 201.7 23

ISBN 13: 978-81-246-0805-0

First published in India in 2015

Published by:
Nalanda International
"Nalanda", 6418, Spring Park Avenue
Los Angeles, CA - 90056 (USA)
Phones: (310)-430-8057; *Fax*: (213)-341 0156
Web: www.nalandainternational.com

and

D.K. Printworld (P) Ltd.
Regd. Office : *'Vedaśrī'*, F-395, Sudarshan Park
(Metro Station: Ramesh Nagar), New Delhi - 110 015
Phones : (011) 2545 3975; 2546 6019; *Fax* : (011) 2546 5926
E-mail : indology@dkprintworld.com
Web : www.dkprintworld.com

Printed by: D.K. Printworld (P) Ltd., New Delhi

In memory of
Ken, Kathy and Billy

Contents

Introduction

Out of the intermingled multitude, almost daily forced into each other's company, there is born a true love for persons of all nationalities so that, coming together with a certain delight, they explore more wisely the true and common good.

– Juan de Segovia in Biechler 2004: 281*

Everything from ruler, minister, husband, wife, and friends to mountains, rivers, spiritual beings, birds, animals, and plants should be truly loved in order to realize my humanity that forms one body with them, and then my clear character will be completely manifested, and I will really form one body with Heaven, Earth, and the myriad things.

– Wang Yang-ming in Chan 1969: 661**

From the Silk Road to the Internet

ONE night in 629 CE, a young Chinese Buddhist named Xuanzang set out alone across the shifting sands of the

---

* Juan de Segovia (1393–1458) was a theologian at the University of Salamanca who translated the Qur'an into Latin from a Spanish translation by a Muslim scholar. After the fall of Constantinople in 1453, he and Cardinal Nicholas of Cusa advocated dialogue between Christian and Islamic leaders instead of a crusade.

** Wang Yang-ming (1472–1529) was a major figure in the development of Neo-Confucianism, a reformulation of Confucian doctrines stimulated by the introduction of Buddhism into China. Wang believed that the "heart/mind possesses an intuitive knowledge which manifests innate wisdom" and that "everyone has sagehood within" (Yao 2000: 112).

Taklamakan Desert beyond the border of the Tang Empire. His destination was India. To reach it he had first to go west; but travel to those troubled regions of Central Asia was restricted by imperial decree. Keeping off the beaten path to avoid detection, he soon lost his way. He collapsed from dehydration before reaching the first oasis and barely survived the desert crossing at the beginning of his pilgrimage.

Sixteen years later, Xuanzang returned to China at the end of a 10,000-mile journey. He had traversed some of the most formidable terrain on earth and criss-crossed the Indian subcontinent acquainting himself with the various schools of Buddhist philosophy. He had studied and taught at Nālandā, one of Asia's foremost centers of learning. King Harṣa, ruler of northern India, had showered him with gifts and honors. Now he was accompanied by a train of horses loaded with hundreds of manuscripts of Buddhist texts he wished to translate. When he reached Chang'an (modern Xi'an), the Tang capital and the largest city in the world, crowds thronged the streets to greet him. The emperor Taizong, whom he had disobeyed when he left China, welcomed him and sought information about the lands he had visited.[1]

Xuanzang's epic journey became the stuff of Chinese legend. It was also a significant episode in the centuries-long spread of Buddhism from India to China. The political scientist Samuel Huntington, best known for his stress on conflict in the relations among civilizations, called this transmission "perhaps the most important cultural diffusion not the result of conquest".[2] Xuanzang's story, along with those of other agents in this peaceful process, provides a vivid historical illustration of the ability of cultures to overcome the barriers that separate them and learn from each other's values and achievements.

---

1 Wriggins 2004: 2-18, 120-26, 160-65, 186-91.

2 Huntington 1997: 49.

Xuanzang's journey was possible because of the Silk Road, a system of routes that enabled the exchange of goods and ideas between far-flung regions of Asia, Europe and sub-Saharan Africa for over a millennium. Travel has become easier since those days. Access to the riches of another culture no longer normally requires a scholar, artist or seeker to risk his or her life as the Chinese monk did in the seventh century. Getting from one place to another is likely to be a matter of hours where it used to take months, if one was lucky. Nor do handwritten copies of documents have to be transported on horses or elephants at the risk of losing some of them in a river as Xuanzang did. Their electronic images can now be flashed over the Internet in a moment to the other side of the earth.

Yet the difficulties Xuanzang faced did not prevent what globalization scholar Nayan Chanda refers to as "the biggest information transfer of the epoch".[3] Dazzling technological advances often blind us to continuities in the dynamics of cultural interchange from ancient to modern times. These continuities are highlighted by the French-born Chinese–American cellist Yo-Yo Ma when he calls the Silk Road "the Internet of antiquity".[4] The difference between then and now is largely a matter of the speed, range and volume of transactions. But the world was more connected in the first millennium than most of us are aware.

Major cultural exchanges once occurred without the benefit of modern technology to facilitate them. On the other hand, our possession of this technology does not guarantee its use for better purposes than those for which our ancestors relied

---

[3] Chanda 2007: 116.

[4] The Silk Road Ensemble directed by Yo-Yo Ma is inspired by the "age-old tradition of cross-cultural exchange" that the Silk Road represents (The Silk Road Project, accessed on 26 September 2014, http://archive.silkroadproject.org/Education/TheSilkRoad/tabid/175/Default.aspx).

on horses and elephants. The Xuanzang of the twentieth century was a Chinese scholar named Xu Fancheng. He lived in India for thirty-three years, spending most of that time at the Sri Aurobindo Ashram, Pondicherry, where he is remembered as Hu Hsu. It goes without saying that his travels were infinitely less eventful than those of his seventh-century predecessor. However, his Chinese translations of texts of Indian spiritual philosophy, ranging from the Upaniṣads to Sri Aurobindo, form a body of work comparable to Xuanzang's.[5]

Xu Fancheng was almost unknown during his lifetime. It is only since his death in Beijing in 2000 that his reputation has begun to grow. In contrast, Xuanzang's funeral more than thirteen centuries earlier is said to have been attended by over a million people.[6] Modernized societies evidently do not value philosophy and spirituality as some ancient civilizations once did. In the near future, whatever revival of cultural contact between China and India may be stimulated by contributions such as Xu Fancheng's is likely to be overshadowed by the more mundane preoccupations of these two mega-countries. China has recently proposed to resurrect the "Southern Silk Road" leading to South Asia – not the route Xuanzang took, but one further east. However beneficial for trade, it cannot be expected to have much immediate cultural impact.

But a short-term view may be misleading. Both India and China are still dealing culturally with the transition to modernity. Though their economic and political power is on the rise and that of the West has begun to wane, Western culture remains globally dominant. Under these circumstances, any challenger's first concern must be not only to recover its

5 Nuo 2009.

6 Wriggins 2004: 210.

own identity, but to assimilate what it needs or wants to take from the West. As the historian William McNeill points out, "one of the clearest patterns in world history" is that "any geographical displacement of world leadership must be prefaced by successful borrowing from previously established centers of the highest prevailing skills".[7] At the moment it is still mainly in the West that those skills are located. Paradoxically, the "Westernization" of Asia may be a sign that Asia is preparing to throw off its subordination to the West. Once that is done, Asian cultures will develop in a new context in which their relations with each other may assume an importance equal to or exceeding what they had in the past.

The religious scholar Xinzhong Yao sums up the attitude of the twentieth-century Neo-Confucian thinker Tang Junyi toward China's adoption of elements of Western culture:

> Accepting and transforming these western elements, while responding to their challenges as well as transcending their limits will enable Chinese culture to be rebuilt in a new system, like the ancient Chinese who created a new system of Buddhism in accepting and transforming Indian Buddhism. Therefore, to reform Chinese culture does not necessarily require the abandonment of its traditions. Returning to the tradition (*fan ben*) and developing the new (*kai xin*) are related and mutually promoted.[8]

Centuries of cultural contact with India played a major role in shaping the Chinese tradition. We may expect a renewal of this contact to be part of the creative return to that tradition.

What is ironic about the present cultural apathy in relations between India and China is that outward conditions are ripe for a far more vibrant interchange than ever before, not only between these two civilizations, but among all the cultures of

---

7 McNeill 1991: xxviii.

8 Yao 2000: 257.

the world. There could be a global renaissance. Since the eighteenth century our species has called itself *homo sapiens* (wise man). In former times, however, the pursuit of wisdom was often taken much more seriously than it is today. The contrast between the recognition received by Xuanzang and Xu Fancheng illustrates the difference between then and now in the case of two cultures where learning and knowledge were traditionally held in the highest esteem. It remains to be seen how far humanity's deepening existential crisis will compel it to grapple once again with the ultimate questions of life.

The Changing Face of Globalization

Globalization is usually assumed to be the result of the surge of Western progress and expansion that began with the Age of Discovery and the Scientific Revolution and has culminated in the Information Age. But globalizing tendencies had already been at work for centuries during Europe's Dark Ages when Xuanzang was traveling the Silk Road, Islam was surging out of the Arabian Peninsula, classical Indian civilization was at its peak and China was the leader in technology. The rise of the West amplified and accelerated economic, political and cultural processes that had long been interlinking much of Afro-Eurasia, if not other continents. It also distorted these processes by associating them anomalously with the dominance of one civilization over all others. That dominance appears to be coming to an end.[9] Globalization continues.

As a corrective to Eurocentric assumptions, it is useful to recognize a premodern phase of globalization. Beginning over 5,000 years ago, according to some scholars, it encompassed

---

9 The realization that the West no longer owns or rules the world – or will not continue to do so for much longer – is reflected in a number of books published in recent years, e.g. Frank 1998; Prestowitz 2005; Meredith 2007; Mahbubani 2008; Jacques 2012; Kupchan 2012; Zakaria 2012.

most of history as a process of slowly and unevenly growing interconnectedness.[10] By the early fourteenth century, before it was disrupted by the Black Death and other factors, an incipient "world system" stretched from Europe to China. It did not include the Americas and Australia and therefore "was not a *global* system", as the sociologist Janet Abu-Lughod explains, but "it represented a substantially larger system than the world had previously known". Its significance to us today is that "it contained no single hegemonic power", so it "provides an important contrast to the world system that grew out of it: the one Europe reshaped to its own ends and dominated for so long".[11]

Around the time of Columbus, the West started to make an increasing impact on the rest of humankind. This peaked during the nineteenth and twentieth centuries. But as Western pre-eminence reached its height, the first signs of a reversal could already be seen. The premodern phase of globalization is important to understand because its postmodern phase may restore, under altered conditions, a multicultural equilibrium such as preceded the ascendancy of the West.

Mountains, deserts and oceans once isolated large masses of humanity from each other to a considerable degree. Contact and mutual influence occurred nevertheless, but geographical conditions were more conducive on the whole to cultural differentiation than to convergence. The separateness imposed

---

10 As the field of globalization studies matures there is a trend toward enlarging its scope. So far there is no consensus about how far to go in this direction. The political theorist Manfred Steger summarizes several viewpoints including the position favored in the present book, which is "that any truly comprehensive account of globalization falls woefully short without the incorporation of ancient developments and enduring dynamics into our planetary history" (Steger 2003: 19).

11 Abu-Lughod 1989: 352-53, 4, 6. Italics in original.

by geography was often reinforced by a tendency to regard those who were different as inferior. They were barbarians, heathen, Mlecchas. As the historian Felipe Fernández-Armesto remarks, "civilizations have usually been contemptuous of most of their neighbors".[12] Even Xuanzang encountered in India a certain amount of prejudice against the Chinese,[13] while Buddhism was vulnerable to sporadic persecution in China on account of its foreign origins. Such attitudes have by no means disappeared, but they are less acceptable today than even 100 years ago. While distinctive civilizations were evolving along largely independent lines whose intersection – fruitful as it may have been – was more the exception than the rule, cultural chauvinism seems to have been almost the norm.

The legacy of the premodern millennia is our multicultural world. Both the problems and the potentials implicit in cultural diversity have been heightened by closer interactions in an age of accelerated globalization. In this book, I will suggest that the advantages of this diversity may outweigh the challenges it poses; I will explore especially what India might contribute to a global culture no longer dominated by the West. But the solution of problems and the realization of potentials will depend on human attitudes, efforts and choices.

Today, geographical barriers have lost much of their power to obstruct the flow of people and ideas. Other barriers persist, including political, linguistic and other obstacles not unlike those that confronted Xuanzang. The world is still only semi-globalized. But many forces are at work to undermine the remaining impediments to movement and communication. Due to this increasing interdependence, human unity in some sense has become for the first time a meaningful prospect. At the

---

12 Fernández-Armesto 2001: 25.

13 Wriggins 2004: xv.

same time, the globalization of modernity seems to have upset an organic balance in the relations of human societies with each other and with nature. Disaster could lie ahead unless a new balance can be established on another basis. We cannot expect this to happen by itself. It requires a clear vision of where we are, how we got here, and where we want to go.

Medea's Cauldron

We live in exhilarating and unnerving times. Whatever country we call home, whatever language or languages we speak, whatever religion we practice, if any, and whether we are educated or illiterate, affluent or destitute, we share with all others a shrinking earth where runaway change seems to be the only constant. The promises and perils of an era of rapid change were encapsulated by the early twentieth-century Indian philosopher Sri Aurobindo in a graphic image from Greek mythology:

> The world today presents the aspect of a huge cauldron of Medea in which all things are being cast, shredded into pieces, experimented on, combined and recombined either to perish and provide the scattered material of new forms or to emerge rejuvenated and changed for a fresh term of existence.[14]

According to legend, the sorceress Medea could restore the youth of one whose dismembered body she stirred in her cauldron. Pelias, her enemy, did not survive the process. For the last 200 or 300 years at least, societies, traditions, institutions, religions and civilizations around the world have been subjected to the disruptive forces of modernity and mixed together more and more furiously in the cauldron of globalization. They may come out with a new lease on life or cease to exist in a recognizable form, perishing like Pelias.

---

14 Aurobindo 2005: 5.

What will emerge from the cauldron? The only certainty is that nothing will remain just as it was. If we imagine a sort of super-Medea at work, we see that her method is both destructive and creative. It involves fragmentation as well as integration. The optimistic, pessimistic or intermediate expectations entertained by hyper-globalists, anti-globalists, and others in between, depend on their perceptions of the relative strength of the positive and negative aspects of what is happening. While no metaphor can capture the complexity of a worldwide transformation, some of these contradictory aspects are evoked by the image of Medea and her cauldron.

Theories of globalization differ in their understanding of the nature of human diversity and the power of the forces that sustain or undermine it. Their predictions of the shape of things to come contrast accordingly. The sociologist Jan Nederveen Pieterse distinguishes three major perspectives. Briefly, *cultural differentialism* claims that "differences are lasting". Proponents of *cultural convergence* hold, on the contrary, that "they yield to growing homogenization". A third view (favored by Nederveen Pieterse himself) is *cultural hybridization*, which argues that "they mix, generating new differences in the process".[15] This summary of the main alternatives suggests three possible interpretations of what is happening in the global cauldron. Each implies a corresponding expectation of the most likely outcome.

Cultural differentialism stresses the vitality and tenacity of the particular identities that distinguish groups from each other. It is a position that appears to have plenty of empirical support in this time of retribalization. Yet it may ultimately overestimate the obstacles to transformative interchange. In its more uncompromising forms, this model offers no remedy for the proneness of dissimilar communities to mutual

---

15 Nederveen Pieterse 2009: 44.

incomprehension, distrust and antagonism. An alarmist outlook on the future is a natural corollary. Medea's cauldron becomes Pandora's box, a matrix of chaos spewing forth ethnic hatreds, regional rivalries and violent fundamentalisms. Apprehensions about where this will lead, however exaggerated at times, cannot be lightly dismissed in our post-9/11 era. We now celebrate diversity, yet cultural barriers can frustrate communication and derail attempts to solve pressing problems. They may not have mattered so much when distances were great and contacts limited; but in a shrinking world of dwindling resources, allegedly unbridgeable cultural divisions compounding other causes of conflict would seem to spell catastrophe.

Convergence theories propose an opposite and at first sight far more benign conception of the global cauldron as a melting pot. In this reinvention of the once popular symbol of American assimilationism, cultural globalization is seen as a homogenizing process where diversity, if not abolished, is trivialized or its consequences neutralized. Dissipating the nightmarish vision conjured up by extreme differentialism, this scenario anticipates a growing sameness of world-views and lifestyles which would reduce causes of friction. On the other hand, the loss of the richness and vigor of human life that might occur in a more uniform world could turn out to be a high price to pay for this otherwise attractive "end of history".

The notion of convergence, as usually formulated, is also haunted by the shadow of imperialism. The swallowing up of other cultures by that of the West began under colonialism and has continued in some directions under the neocolonial ideology of market globalism. But this is far from being the whole picture and it is debatable whether it is still the predominant trend. As the non-Western world increasingly asserts itself, there is less and less reason to believe that a convergence on values and institutions derived from European culture is humanity's destiny.

Cultural convergence would progressively weaken and eventually dissolve the boundaries that preoccupy the differentialists. But if we look at today's realities, what we see is neither a world of entirely separate cultural entities colliding like billiard balls nor a merging of diverse societies into a shapeless monoculture of global modernity. The opposing models of differentialism and convergence seem equally one-sided and incomplete. Each overstates an aspect of the relationship of cultures to each other as distinct yet interacting and to some extent interpenetrating units. Neither model in isolation appears to be fully sustainable. Therefore a third position has recently gained adherents among scholars. The concept of hybridity offers a way of accepting the permeability of boundaries without sacrificing variety to homogenizing or hegemonic forces. In this view of cultural change, influences flow both ways and whatever diversity is lost is constantly replaced in an ongoing process.

Something Torn and New

Of the three alternatives, the hybridity model corresponds most closely to the metaphor we began with. In Medea's cauldron, as we have seen it interpreted by Sri Aurobindo to symbolize the creative destruction unleashed by modernity, all things are being intensively "combined and recombined" – a definition of hybridization – with the prospect that what remains intact will "emerge rejuvenated and changed". In that case, the promise made by the sorceress in the legend to lure her victim into undergoing dismemberment may be fulfilled after all. For all the ghastliness of the operation, the global cauldron may yet turn out to be a fountain of youth. What emerges from it may be – in a phrase of the poet Kamau Brathwaite, used by Ngũgĩ wa Thiong'o as the title of a book on the African renaissance – "something torn and new".[16]

---

16 Brathwaite 1973: 270.

Ngũgĩ points out the role of dismemberment in the methods of colonialism and especially in the subjugation and exploitation of Africa, which suffered the atrocities of the slave trade in addition to being divided up among several European powers. In this context he comments on the fascination of African writers with the story of Osiris, another myth of dismemberment and re-membering.[17] Such an image would naturally resonate with those who have experienced both the brutality of colonialism and the resilience of societies subjected to it. This resilience might seem to support the view that cultural identities and the differences that constitute them are inextinguishable. But these identities are not static. Cultures change through contact with each other, even when identities are preserved. The contribution of hybridization theory has been to highlight this process of reciprocal modification.

Cultural purity is a myth. The economist Tyler Cowen comments on the mixed composition of civilizations:

> The very foundations of the West (and other civilizations throughout history) are multicultural products, resulting from the international exchange of goods, services, and ideas. To varying degrees, Western cultures draw their philosophical heritage from the Greeks, their religions from the Middle East, their scientific base from the Chinese and Islamic worlds, and their core populations and languages from Europe.[18]

Along the same lines, Sri Aurobindo notes that Greek civilization itself had developed "under the influence of Egyptian, Phoenician and other oriental influences" before it "separated itself sharply from the non-Hellenic 'barbarian'

---

[17] Ngũgĩ 2009: 33-36. "Re-membering" is used figuratively in the sense of reconstituting what was fragmented as well as recovering conscious connection with the past.

[18] Cowen 2002: 6.

cultures".[19] Even France, with its strong sense of national unity, he analyzes into its original constituents as an "old Gallic nation with its Basque, Gaelic, Armorican and other ancient elements modified by the Frank and Latin admixture".[20] Historical instances of such mixing could be multiplied indefinitely.

On an individual level, Aurobindo himself was an example of the cultural intermingling he describes. Given his upbringing, it is no surprise that he alludes to a Greek myth in the sentence quoted earlier from a book written in English to contribute to a spiritual renewal in India. He spent most of his formative years in England, studying European history and literature and winning prizes in Greek and Latin at Cambridge. On his return to India he underwent a process of indigenization and emerged for a few years as an early leader of the country's freedom struggle. He identified himself for some time as a Hindu, but kept a breadth of outlook which asserted itself strongly in writings such as *The Ideal of Human Unity* and *The Human Cycle*. Along with Swami Vivekananda, another central figure in the intellectual and spiritual history of modern India, he will recur throughout this book as a non-Western contributor to the conversation. A third historically important voice from India will be that of another Westernized intellectual blending nationalism with cosmopolitanism, Jawaharlal Nehru, one of the architects of the country's independence and its first prime minister.

"Aurobindo was a hybrid", an American professor of religious studies once told me to explain the relative lack of academic interest in this remarkable thinker. I was puzzled. Shouldn't that be a plus? Orientalist nostalgia for the exotic is perhaps an understandable defense against the flood of hybridity engulfing us, but it may be doubted how much a

---

19 Aurobindo 2004: 50.

20 Aurobindo 1998b: 39.

quixotic pursuit of cultural purity will illuminate the complex realities of our time.

Be that as it may, what questions one asks and where one looks for the answers are undoubtedly shaped by biographical factors. For this reason Nederveen Pieterse begins his *Globalization and Culture* with an account of his Eurasian, hybrid origins in a Dutch East Indies colonial family. "I don't mention this because I think it is unusual," he clarifies, "but rather because I think it is common: one way or another, we are all migrants."[21] Similarly, I could mention my own background as an American of German, Irish, Norwegian and Icelandic ancestry who have spent half of my life in India, where I now live. The meeting and intertwining of civilizations – usually harmonious and mutually beneficial, occasionally more problematic – frames my daily existence.

Cruising on the Seas of Time

My personal experience largely accounts for the issues chosen for discussion in these essays. My treatment of these issues, on the other hand, will not be first-person or anecdotal. It will be historical and comparative, interdisciplinary but non-technical. By historical I do not mean that I write as a professional historian. My approach has more in common with philosophy of history than with historiography proper. But I have exercised liberally three capacities which, according to John Gaddis, distinguish historians from other time travelers:

> Historians have the capacity for selectivity, simultaneity, and the shifting of scale: they can select from the cacophony of events what they think is really important; they can be in several times and places at once; and they can zoom in and out between macroscopic and microscopic levels of analysis.[22]

---

21 Nederveen Pieterse 2009: 3.

22 Gaddis 2002: 22.

In particular, I have singled out from the "cacophony" of recorded events one relatively neglected by historians, whose significance I have tried to bring out from various points of view. This is the Parliament of Religions held in Chicago in 1893, best known in some circles for the fact that it launched the public career of Swami Vivekananda. In my discussions of this and other events, I will often "zoom in and out between macroscopic and microscopic levels of analysis", placing these events in contexts such as globalization and the distinction made in religious studies between exclusivism, inclusivism and pluralism in attitudes toward differences in belief and practice. In so doing, I will at times skim through history in a manner which can perhaps best be justified by citing the words of the historian of the *longue durée*, Fernand Braudel:

> This long-term history, history-at-a-distance – blue-water cruising on the high seas of time, rather than prudent coastal navigation never losing sight of land – this way of proceeding, call it what you will, has both advantages and drawbacks. Its advantages are that it forces one to think, to explain matters in unaccustomed terms, and to use historical explanation as a key to one's own time.[23]

For this kind of cruising through world history, "civilizations" are a useful concept. A civilization is defined by Huntington as "the broadest cultural entity" or, more precisely, "the broadest level of cultural identity people have short of that which distinguishes humans from other species".[24] As is shown by the debates over Huntington's well-known book, *The Clash of Civilizations and the Remaking of World Order*, this way of subdividing humanity has its problems. But I believe that these problems arise mainly when we see civilizations from a perspective of cultural differentialism, demarcating too rigidly

---

23 Braudel 1993: 35.

24 Huntington 1997: 43.

the boundaries between them and underestimating the creative potential of their interactions. I have tried to suggest this potential by substituting "clasp" for "clash" while echoing Huntington's phrase in the title of the present book.[25]

Boundaries exist, of course, and they help to preserve the diversity that gives human life much of its interest and vitality. But these boundaries are often highly permeable and this diversity is not, nor has it ever been, immutable. We have seen this in the case of China's acceptance of Buddhism from India. Buddhism's spiritual individualism made an impact on the communal Confucian ethos and was assimilated in Neo-Confucianism. But China remained as Chinese as ever. Even Buddhism was Sinicized in China and never became a replica of Indian Buddhism.

Braudel speaks of "basic values" and "psychological structures" which "are assuredly the features that civilizations can least easily communicate one to another. They are what isolate and differentiate them most sharply. And such habits of mind survive the passage of time. They change little, and change slowly." Yet they do change, both from within and through interaction with other civilizations:

> Civilizations continually borrow from their neighbours, even if they "reinterpret" and assimilate what they have adopted. . . . Just as a civilization may welcome or refuse elements from another civilization, so it may accept or reject survivals from its own past. It does so slowly, and almost

25 An internet search for the phrase "clasp of civilizations" shows that a few others have used it, usually in passing. The most relevant instance is the lecture "Islam and Christianity: Clash or Clasp of Civilizations" delivered by the historian William Dalrymple in Cairo in November 2006 (website of the Church of St John the Baptist accessed on 26 September 2014, http://www.stjohnschurchmaadi.org/learning-and-lectures#!_learning-and-lectures/vstc1=william-dalrymple).

> always unconsciously or partly so. In this way, it gradually transforms itself.[26]

The pace of change itself can change, however, at a time of extraordinary upheaval such as we are passing through today. Thrown into the global cauldron, distinctive civilizations have remained intact to a greater degree than modernization theorists once thought possible; but powerful homogenizing forces have also been at work. The likely fate of cultural differences under these circumstances is concisely summarized by globalization scholar Pankaj Ghemawat:

> The cultural tableau that spreads out before us includes cultural differences or barriers that won't change anytime soon, as well as cultural differences that *will* fade, albeit to a more limited extent than one might expect, and other differences that will evolve instead of dissolving.[27]

These three possibilities correspond to the three perspectives on globalization discussed earlier: cultural differentialism, convergence and hybridization (assuming that the evolution of differences is catalyzed by interchange). But instead of being treated as conflicting theoretical alternatives, these descriptions are applied here to simultaneous processes that can be studied in the past, observed in the present and projected into the future.

Evolving Differences

Differences "that won't change anytime soon" and those "that *will* fade" have in recent years been stressed, respectively, by Samuel Huntington and Francis Fukuyama. As the proponents of two of the most controversial analyses of the post-Cold War world, their views are often portrayed in terms of a diametric opposition which Fukuyama himself considers

26 Braudel 1993: 22, 29, 31.

27 Ghemawat 2011: 228.

exaggerated. Setting aside common misrepresentations of both positions, however, the contrast between *The Clash of Civilizations* and *The End of History* provides a starting point for considering a third option which emphasizes differences "that will evolve instead of dissolving".

While Huntington and Fukuyama may agree more than is usually recognized, the latter acknowledges a fundamental issue separating his vision from that of his former teacher:

> It is the question of whether the values and institutions developed during the Western Enlightenment are *potentially* universal (as Hegel and Marx thought), or bounded within a cultural horizon (consistent with the views of later philosophers like Nietzsche and Heidegger). Huntington clearly believes that they are not universal.

The institution whose universality Fukuyama is most keen to establish is democracy. In this regard he goes on to state his view as opposed to that of Huntington:

> Huntington is quite correct when he says that the *historical* origin of modern secular liberal democracy lies in Christianity. . . . But while modern liberal democracy has its roots in this particular cultural soil, the issue is whether these ideas may become detached from these particularistic origins and have a significance for people who live in non-Christian cultures. . . . I believe that this is the case, and I think that there is an overall logic to historical evolution that explains why there should be increasing democracy around the world as our societies evolve.[28]

One can agree with Fukuyama that it is possible for ideas developed in a specific cultural context to become detached from their origins and incorporated in other cultures (though this may not make them universal). History would have been very different if this had never happened. On the other hand,

[28] Fukuyama 2006: 342-43.

there is no reason to suppose that only occidental ideas can be so transplanted. Fukuyama may be right in the long run about the spread of democracy. This is surely one of the West's most significant contributions. But it would betray a failure of imagination to believe that democratization, even if complete and universal, would bring historical evolution to an end. This is often assumed to be Fukuyama's position. His actual view was more nuanced. He concluded the first edition of *The End of History* with the image of global democratization as a wagon train heading toward a common destination. Even "provided a majority of the wagons eventually reach the same town", he admitted, in the final analysis we cannot know "whether their occupants, having looked around a bit at their new surroundings, will not find them inadequate and set their eyes on a new and more distant journey".[29]

In contrast to Fukuyama, Huntington points out the "decreasing relevance and usefulness" of "monocivilizational viewpoints" in a "multicivilizational world".[30] Yet the success of his attempt to remove his own monocivilizational blinkers is questionable. Political theory remains Eurocentric, by and large, despite a growing uneasiness about this limitation.

Among non-Western thinkers offering a distinctive perspective, Sri Aurobindo has so far been neglected by most scholars. But as the Indian historian Sugata Bose observes, Aurobindo has "shown that in the domain of creating a state Indian nationalism was not condemned to pirating from the gallery of models crafted by the West".[31] For the sake of a broader discussion of an issue of global importance, it may be of interest to consider what Sri Aurobindo has to say about democracy as a stage in the evolution of societies:

---

29 Fukuyama 2006: 339.

30 Huntington 1997: 55.

31 Bose 2013: 126.

> Certainly, democracy as it is now practised is not the last or penultimate stage; for it is often merely democratic in appearance and even at the best amounts to the rule of the majority. . . . Even a perfect democracy is not likely to be the last stage of social evolution, but it is still the necessary broad standing-ground upon which the self-consciousness of the social being can come to its own.

This assessment of the merits and limits of democracy is distinctly unconcerned with problems of cultural adaptation. In this respect Aurobindo supports Fukuyama, but with reservations about the adequacy of any political ideology. Coming to specifics of the machinery of government, he elaborates:

> Parliamentarism, the invention of the English political genius, is a necessary stage in the evolution of democracy, for without it the generalised faculty of considering and managing with the least possible friction large problems of politics, administration, economics, legislation concerning considerable aggregates of men cannot easily be developed. It has also been the one successful means yet discovered of preventing the State executive from suppressing the liberties of the individual and the nation. Nations emerging into the modern form of society are therefore naturally and rightly attracted to this instrument of government.[32]

Despite this pragmatic endorsement, Sri Aurobindo can hardly be called a harbinger of Fukuyama's celebration of secular liberal democracy as the fulfilment of the evolutionary logic of history. In some ways, substantial differences notwithstanding, his overall vision has more in common with Huntington's insistence on the independence of non-Western civilizations, which if they accept Western ideas can be expected to do so in their own manner and for their own reasons.

---

[32] Aurobindo 1998b: 456-57, 472-73.

In an essay on "Indian Culture and External Influence", Sri Aurobindo discusses the adoption in India of European social, political and other innovations. He looks at the question in relation to the process of cultural interchange in general rather than in terms of any universal value of Western civilization as such – for if these ideas are worth accepting, "it is not because they are modern or European, which is in itself no recommendation". The principles involved in such interchange are the same for the group as for the individual. On the one hand, "it is neither desirable nor possible to exclude everything that comes in to us from outside"; on the other, "a living organism . . . must recast the things it takes in to suit the law and form and characteristic action of its biological or psychological body".[33]

An external impact may evoke one or more of three responses. It "may act as an irritant" which is rejected; but "in this process of rejection there is some resultant of change and growth". Or it "may act as a stimulus, awakening a new action of the self-consciousness and a sense of fresh possibility". Or else it may "come in as a possible material which has then to be reshaped to a form of the inner energy, harmonised with the inner being". When there is a bombardment of such impacts – as there was in India under colonialism, the context of Sri Aurobindo's essay, and as there is everywhere today due to globalization – the various responses to these materials, irritants and stimuli may occur simultaneously:

> In a great change of environment or a close meeting with a mass of invading influences all these processes work together and there is possibly much temporary perplexity and difficulty, . . . but also the opportunity of a great self-developing transformation or an immense and vigorous renascence.[34]

---

33 Aurobindo 2004: 47-48.

34 Aurobindo 2004: 49-50.

Ex Oriente Lux

The last few centuries have witnessed the dramatic entrance onto the world stage of a group of nations that rather suddenly emerged from the backwater of medieval Europe. Armed with science and technology made possible by borrowings from their hitherto more advanced contemporaries, these upstarts managed to break down the relative isolation of continents and impose their own power and influence on much of humanity. If they had not turned against each other and nearly destroyed themselves in two gigantic wars, they might have succeeded in remaking the world in their own image. But in the middle decades of the twentieth century, decolonization put an end to the direct political domination of the West over "the Rest". Economic domination has lasted longer, with the center of power transferred from Europe to America; but this is also eroding.

Every society on earth continues to be subjected to the impact of the modern way of life as it has taken shape in the West. Each must work out its own response to it. What cannot be sustained much longer is the attempt to claim a unique and privileged status for values supposed to be of Western origin. As the West becomes one civilization among others in a multicultural world, it no longer has any semblance of control over the forces it has let loose. Whatever the risk of chaos, the advantage of this state of affairs is that the inputs of all cultures are pooled together, opening up incalculable prospects for the future.

Cultural globalization is no longer synonymous with Westernization or – as it seemed for a while – Americanization. Reversals in the direction of influence have led some scholars to speak of alternative globalizations. In the introduction to *Many Globalizations: Cultural Diversity in the Contemporary World*, the sociologist Peter Berger (co-editor with Samuel Huntington) observes:

> Arguably the most important cultural influence coming from Asia into the West . . . arrives in the form of the so-called New Age culture. It has affected millions of people in Europe and America, both on the level of beliefs (reincarnation, karma, the mystical connections between the individual and all of nature) and of behavior.

Berger draws a parallel with the late Roman period, when "in circles dissatisfied with what Greco-Roman civilization had to offer, there was a turn toward the East in terms of behavior and ideas – *ex oriente lux*. In the end, the West Asian movement of Christianity was the greatest beneficiary of this cultural development."[35] In later centuries, this Asian religion in a modified form became the basis of European civilization. Eventually it was secularized and transformed into the values underlying modern political ideologies. These were then exported to the rest of the world through imperialism and globalization.

It is too soon to predict whether the influence of Asian spirituality on the modern West will have equally far-reaching consequences. Much will depend on how Asia itself evolves. In any case, this component of the New Age movement represents only the most recent phase of a long-term phenomenon. During a previous phase in the early nineteenth century, notes the intellectual historian J.J. Clarke, the German philosopher Schopenhauer believed "that the influx of Indian ideas into Europe represented a new Renaissance which would bring about a fundamental transformation in European thought, a transformation of far greater impact than that of Europe on Asia".[36] So far no such transformation has occurred. But given the present Asian resurgence under conditions of intensified intercultural contact and planetary crisis, the wave

---

35 Berger and Huntington 2002: 13-14. *Ex oriente lux* can be translated "light out of the East".

36 Clarke 1997: 69.

from the East seems less likely to peter out than to continue gaining momentum and assuming new forms.

There is no reason, however, to expect that masses of Westerners will ever adopt old or new Eastern religions exactly as practiced in Asia. Civilizations, as Braudel has told us, reinterpret and assimilate what they borrow. Christianity itself was Europeanized as much as Europe was Christianized. The New Age culture has likewise Westernized and, notoriously, commercialized much that it has received from the East. At the same time, we would miss its real significance if we make this an excuse for dismissing all it stands for. New Age thinkers, Clarke observes, "are convinced of the spiritual bankruptcy of the West, and have been prepared to draw syncretistically on Eastern as well as Western symbols and concepts to provide a new overarching philosophical framework". They have used "Eastern thought in pursuit of a fundamental rethinking of the Western intellectual tradition".[37] In this respect they have followed in the footsteps of eighteenth-century Enlightenment sinophiles, nineteenth-century romantic orientalists, and others in the long history of East–West cultural interchange.

Current critiques of orientalist scholarship up to the mid-twentieth century tend to reduce it to a rationalization of colonial power. This interpretation is applicable to some of its manifestations, but not to all. As Clarke argues,

> orientalism has for three centuries assumed a counter-cultural, counter-hegemonic role, and become in various ways a gadfly plaguing all kinds of orthodoxies, and an energiser of radical protest, and in doing so it has often been in the business not of reinforcing Europe's established role and identity, but rather of undermining it.[38]

---

37 Clarke 1997: 105, 69.

38 Ibid.: 27.

The New Age movement on its intellectual side has inherited and carried forward this self-critical undercurrent in Western thought.

Reason, Unreason and the Ultrarational

In a long view of history, the East's influence on the West has been no less profound than the West's more recent impact on the East. But the values and institutions developed in the Western Enlightenment, whatever their origin and destiny, are the single most powerful cultural force in the world today. The Enlightenment claimed to be the age of reason. Reason was, of course, not discovered or invented in seventeenth- and eighteenth-century Europe. But arguably such a thoroughgoing rationalization of society as was then proposed had never been envisioned before or elsewhere. The project of eliminating irrationality from human life promised extraordinary benefits and has partially delivered some of them in the course of a few of the most eventful centuries in history. Yet it has met with setbacks that raise troubling questions about the redemptive power attributed to reason. The disenchantment of the world that seems to be the inevitable consequence of pure rationalism has left many people dissatisfied. It can even be doubted whether the faith in reason itself is entirely rational.

The problem with the single-minded pursuit of rationality was suggested by the theologian Reinhold Niebuhr when he pointed out:

> These same rational forces which bring infrarational forces under control seem also to destroy the ultrarational forces of life.

Excessive rationalism, Niebuhr maintained, undermines our imagination, our poetry, our dreams of a better world and our energy to realize them. He goes on to stress the need to bring "prejudices, bigotries, and impulses under the control of reason" and adds, "there are so many people who suffer from the miseries created by unreason that there are not many people who are willing to admit that anything evil can come out of the cultivation of intelligence or the rational approach to life".[39] But this last observation applies less to the non-Western world, where rationalization of the modern kind has come in the same package with colonization.

A "rational approach to life" is what the West has claimed to offer to humankind. When its offer was not eagerly accepted it has sometimes tried to impose it by force, justifying the disparity between the means and the end as a regrettable necessity of what was once called the West's "civilizing mission" (more recently replaced by the duty to spread the boons of free markets and democracy). Despite these contradictions, modernization as rationalization has undoubtedly changed human life for the better in many ways. At the same time, its limitations and unintended consequences have become increasingly evident.

Rationalism still has adherents who claim that it supersedes and invalidates the religious irrationalism of the past. To many rationalists, the rise of fundamentalism in the last few decades is a sign that religion, in its death throes, is showing its true colors. From their point of view, this reactionary phase is the recrudescence of a remnant of medievalism that sooner or later is sure to exhaust itself, fade into oblivion and, if we are lucky, take all surviving forms of religion with it. For those who are neither rationalists nor fundamentalists, however, the recent religious resurgence has a more complex and ambiguous significance. The outbursts of mass religiosity that the world has witnessed, especially since the 1970s, suggest the inadequacy of secular rationalism and attest to the continuing vitality of religious alternatives. Yet there are

---

39 Rice 1993: 12.

deeply religious people, including many traditionalists in all faiths, who worry that religion is being hijacked by fanatics.

After thousands of years at the center of human life, religion finds itself being pushed to the margins by secularization. It tends to respond either adaptively or militantly, as scholars of fundamentalism have noted, "by assimilating to the values of the secular world or by mobilizing in opposition to this invasion and to the traitors who compromise with the enemy".[40] The adaptive response risks rationalizing, subjectivizing and privatizing religion and spirituality out of existence. Taking up arms against the modern world, on the other hand, is not a constructive alternative. Religion fails in both cases to make the best use of its real strength: the urge toward transcendence. Otherwise believers would neither feel threatened by rationalism and materialism nor succumb to their lures. Not repelled or seduced by these modern trends but looking beyond them, the spiritual person should be able, as Sri Aurobindo was, to "observe with respect and wonder the work that Atheism has done for the Divine and admire the services that Agnosticism has rendered in preparing the illimitable increase of knowledge".[41]

Fundamentalist movements have sprung up in various cultural and political settings and differ from each other in many ways. If they have enough in common to describe them with a single (admittedly contested) term, it is because the diffusion of secular modernity has elicited a similar range of reactions everywhere. Among the legacies of the Enlightenment that structure the modern consciousness is a trenchant opposition between the rational and the irrational. Within this framework, religion has basically had two options:

---

40 Almond, Appleby and Sivan 2003: 122.

41 Aurobindo 2005a: 14.

to accommodate itself in one way or another to the rational order of things, or to revolt against that order and see itself identified with the irrational. Simplifying a complex picture, we can say that mainstream religion has chosen the former alternative, fundamentalism the latter.

Fundamentalists confront the secularist discourse of reason vs. unreason with a discourse based on the opposition between God and godlessness, as defined by their own beliefs. While they make use of reason in order to refashion traditional mythologies into religious ideologies suitable for our times, their gestures toward rationality usually impress only believers. Thus they fit neatly into the "irrational" category of secularism's rational/irrational duality. There is no term in common between this dichotomy and that of God/godlessness. But without the minimum amount of common ground needed to agree on what the conflict is about, there is little prospect of meaningful dialogue between religious fundamentalists and secular humanists. In the absence of dialogue, brute force has all too often been called in as the arbiter between their incommensurable claims.

Since secular modernism remains dominant in the global scene, however precariously, it appears that fundamentalism is fighting a losing battle. Yet the hegemony of the rationalist discourse is intrinsically problematic and deserves to be challenged, though not in a fundamentalist manner. Many things inherited from the Enlightenment can and should be questioned, including the simplistic opposition between reason and unreason. However, there is a way to destabilize the rational/irrational binary that might prove far more effective in the long run than the confrontational fundamentalist strategy. It is to accept the opposition between reason and unreason as valid but incomplete and introduce a third term corresponding to Niebuhr's ultrarational. This is sometimes called gnosis.

At least as a hypothetical expansion of our conceptual framework, it is hard to argue against such a move on rational grounds. Perhaps what was wrong with the Enlightenment and its ideology of rational progress was that it was neither enlightened enough nor progressive enough. Fixated on social and political change, it lacked the concepts of spiritual enlightenment and inner progress found in many non-Western cultures (as well as in Western esotericism). Thus it stopped short of an integral vision of the human potential. In contrast, religions such as Hinduism and Buddhism have tended in the past to be socially unprogressive, but are oriented toward an ideal of self-transcendence, enlightenment or liberation to which each individual is invited to aspire through as many incarnations as are needed to achieve it.

Spirit and Intellect: Enemies or Allies?

A recognition of the impulse toward transcendence at the heart of religion could lead to a reassessment of its nature and the role it might play in the future. In this respect, Asian religions have much to offer. As globalization takes an increasingly multicultural turn, Eastern civilizations with their rich heritage of spiritual philosophies and disciplines are reasserting their distinctive identities. They may choose to reconsider how much they want to keep of the type of secularism that has developed in Europe under historical conditions peculiar to that part of the world. At the same time, they need not continue harboring the divisive fundamentalisms that this secularism has cast as its shadows. Religion could then emerge as a forward-looking and transformative rather than regressive and obstructive force in the post-secular world.

Religion and spirituality may owe something of their widespread and persistent hold on humanity to a deep-rooted intuition of a dimension of reality beyond the normal range of the reasoning mind. If latent faculties exist in us whose emergence could enlarge our awareness and extend our means of knowledge, it is hard to see why the progressive intellect should be hostile to their development. In most cultures, the relationship between intellect and spirit has been more cooperative than antagonistic. Even in Western science, though the intellect tends to take credit, many of the paradigm-shifting breakthroughs cannot easily be explained in purely rational terms – nor are they so explained by those who make them, as we will see in the last chapter of this book. The great artistic creations are even more difficult to account for without acknowledging the role of inspiration, often overtly religious.

Over a century ago, Swami Vivekananda spoke to an audience in London of a faculty of knowledge transcending reason:

> Thus, a tremendous statement is made by all religions; that the human mind, at certain moments, transcends not only the limitations of the senses, but also the power of reasoning. It then comes face to face with facts which it could never have sensed, could never have reasoned out. These facts are the basis of all the religions of the world.

Vivekananda added significantly: "Of course we have the right to challenge these facts, to put them to the test of reason."[42] His point was not that the rational intellect is necessarily the most competent judge of all things, but that it must be left free to draw its own conclusions. There may be truths that are more accessible to other, non-rational faculties. But there "cannot be any growth without liberty",[43] he insisted. Today a return to the past by any abrogation of the rational mind's hard-won freedom from dogmatic authority is unlikely to be acceptable for long. On the other hand, it is mere hubris for the intellect to claim that it is the limit of human possibilities and there can be nothing beyond itself.

---

42 Vivekananda 1989, vol. 2: 61.

43 Ibid., vol. 4: 367.

The collaboration of spirit and intellect should be to the advantage of both. An alliance of our most developed capacities of consciousness, rational and suprarational, would fortify both against the siege of the infrarational. The elevation of humankind out of the mud of its evolutionary origins is the ultimate purpose of culture in the higher sense of the word. The mutual embrace and enrichment of diverse civilizations would create the most favorable conditions for an unprecedented flowering of the human mind and spirit on earth.

The Essays

Each of us has an image of the world which structures how we make sense of things. Its content differs according to culture and varies from individual to individual. This image or knowledge structure includes concepts of our location in space and time as well as our relationship to other beings and possibly to other worlds. It determines what we take for fact and implies a scale of values.[44]

As modern individuals, we visualize the earth as a globe spinning through the enormity of space, a comparative speck of matter where life has been evolving for countless aeons. We believe our own newly-emerged species to be for now the highest form of life on our planet. Whether its members are capable of contact with realities beyond their own consciousness, supposing them to exist, is for many an open question. This image of the universe and ourselves is of relatively recent origin. It sets us apart from most of our ancestors, affecting our attitudes and behavior in ways we often take for granted. The growing awareness of the earth as a finite globe and its human occupants as a single community, however diverse and divided, may be called the globalization of consciousness. The development of this

[44] This concept of the image was developed by the economist and systems theorist Kenneth Boulding in a classic study (1956).

perspective is briefly surveyed in "This Little Whirling Globe", the first chapter in the book.

Globalization is usually taken to be a product of the rise of the West. It tends to be perceived as a threat to other cultures. Without minimizing Europe's contribution, this book questions the Western triumphalist view of the global age. An event in the last decade of the nineteenth century, when imperialism was in full swing, was an early sign of the potential impact of the renewed self-assertion of ancient Asian civilizations under modern conditions. This unique event was the World's Parliament of Religions in Chicago. As a landmark in the modern interaction between East and West, it provides a historical focus for reflections on issues pertaining to the past, present and future of cultural and religious diversity that will recur throughout the book. Introduced near the end of the opening chapter, the Parliament's significance is explored in the second chapter, "An Unmanageable Encounter: The Meeting of Religions and Cultures in Chicago, 1893".[45]

Attention then shifts from the late nineteenth century to the present. The consequences of decolonization in the mid-twentieth century were overshadowed for a few decades by the Cold War. As the Indian writer Pankaj Mishra points out, the Western mind has not yet entirely adjusted to the new reality:

> For most people in Europe and America, the history of the twentieth century is still largely defined by the two world wars and the long nuclear stand-off with Soviet Communism. But it is now clearer that the central event of the last century for the majority of the world's population

---

[45] Paper presented at a conference entitled "Swami Vivekananda and the Making of Modern India" held at the Nehru Memorial Museum & Library, New Delhi, 11-12 January 2013. Published as NMML Occasional Paper on History and Society, New Series, no. 22 (2013).

> was the intellectual and political awakening of Asia and its emergence from the ruins of both Asian and European empires.[46]

As the Cold War came to an end, Samuel Huntington was among the first political scientists to ask what the resurgence of non-Western peoples with their own distinctive cultures portended for international relations. His provocative answer is critiqued in the third chapter, "Civilizations and Post-Cold War Conflict".

Discussion of the unresolved controversy stirred up by Huntington continues in the next chapter, "Pluralism and the Clasp of Civilizations". This essay takes up the role of religion in culture, highlighting the tension between its divisive and unifying properties. If civilizations clash, as Huntington feared, religious exclusivism will certainly aggravate conflict. The growth of religious pluralism, on the other hand, could work to defuse cultural antagonisms. The argument for pluralism and its capacity to "grease the wheels" of a complex world, as Swami Vivekananda put it, is made with further reference to the first Parliament of Religions. The capacity to embrace difference is needed today as never before. Globalization has led to a crisis in the world-system and humanity has to choose its destiny. There could be a disastrous clash of civilizations; but Huntington himself, the prophet of this worst-case scenario, gives sensible advice on how to avoid it. If civilizations could "clasp" rather than clash, their diversity might become our most valuable resource.

A civilization that is likely to play a key part in a new world order is singled out in the fifth chapter, "Untold Potentialities: Jawaharlal Nehru, Sri Aurobindo and the Idea of India". Sri Aurobindo and Nehru both played important roles at different stages in the Indian independence movement.

---

46 Mishra 2012: 8.

They are widely, but inaccurately, taken to stand for incompatible concepts of Indian nationhood. As this essay shows, Sri Aurobindo was not the Hindu nationalist he is commonly misrepresented as being. Nor was Nehru a diehard secularist in the anti-religious sense of the word. Sri Aurobindo and Nehru had visions of India that can be seen as complementary rather than conflicting. Both insisted first on the need for freedom and the revitalization of a country demoralized by colonialism. What a liberated and reviving India would do with this freedom is a question which Nehru, as the nation's first prime minister, had to grapple with in immediate practical terms. Sri Aurobindo saw the same question in the context of a large spiritual and evolutionary vision that goes far beyond Nehru's ideas in many respects, but is not fundamentally inconsistent with them.

In the sixth chapter we move around the globe to America, the current leader of Western civilization. America's spiritual contact with India figured in earlier chapters in connection with the Parliament of Religions. This contact has been deepening ever since Vivekananda addressed his "sisters and brothers" in Chicago on 11 September 1893. In "Serenity, Courage and Wisdom: Reinhold Niebuhr, Sri Aurobindo and the American Dream",[47] some reflections on America's history and potential destiny are offered by juxtaposing socio-political ideas of the German–American theologian Reinhold Niebuhr with relevant aspects of the thought of Sri Aurobindo. This essay also analyzes structural similarities between the Protestant minister's Serenity Prayer and features of the Indian

---

[47] Paper presented at a conference entitled "AUM 2010: Manifesting the Spiritual Destiny of America" hosted by the Matagiri Center for the Evolution of Consciousness at Menla Mountain Retreat and Conference Center, Phoenicia, NY, 8-11 July 2010. Published in *Collaboration: Journal of the Integral Yoga of Sri Aurobindo and the Mother*, (Winter 2010/11) **35**(2): 15-23.

mystic's Integral Yoga. These parallels cannot be accounted for by any mutual influence. They are best explained as due to the common spiritual needs of humanity everywhere in the modern world, transcending conventional religious and cultural differences.

The book concludes with a look at the role of intuition as a means of knowledge in both East and West. A rational, objective approach to knowledge has been developed to an unprecedented degree in Western civilization since the Enlightenment. A more intuitive, subjective approach has tended to be characteristic of Eastern cultures. In neither the West nor the East, however, has one approach or the other been exclusively followed. In "Intuition and the Limits of Reason: A Cross-Cultural Study",[48] the role that intuition has played in Western science is discussed as an example of the cooperation of rational and non-rational faculties in some of humanity's most extraordinary achievements, such as the discoveries of quantum physics. Albert Einstein himself, far from opposing science to religion, regarded the true scientific attitude as religious in the highest sense. For a number of leading scientists this quasi-religious outlook has meant an openness to influences from the East. It is typically the original thinkers and creative personalities that have this kind of openness. Lesser minds often erect artificial barriers such as those between religion and science or East and West. But history is on the side of the barrier-breakers.

48 Paper presented at a conference entitled "Consciousness and Knowledge: Scientific and Spiritual Perspectives" organized by the International School for Jain Studies, New Delhi, 11-12 December 2010. Published in *Śraddhā*, **3**(2): 61-77 (2011).

1

This Little Whirling Globe

> *"Global" is above all a space reference, the product of the location of the earth in space, a material celebration of the natural environment on which human beings depend, the evocation of the concrete wholeness or completeness of existence, embracing humanity rather than dividing it.*
>
> – Martin Albrow 1996: 83

The Idea of the Globe

OVER the ages, our consciousness has expanded and the earth has shrunk. Or so it seems if we look at the subjective side of what has recently come to be called globalization. While the economic and other material aspects of globalization have attracted the most attention, some scholars have also commented on its psychological dimension. For the sociologist Roland Robertson, for example,

> Globalization as a concept refers both to the compression of the world and the intensification of consciousness of the world as a whole.[1]

Elaborating on this definition, political scientist Manfred Steger observes that people's "awareness of the receding importance of geographical boundaries and distances fosters a keen sense of becoming part of a global whole. Reinforced on a daily basis, these persistent experiences of global interdependence

---

[1] Robertson 1992: 8.

gradually change people's individual and collective identities, and thus dramatically impact the way they act in the world."[2]

The accelerated globalization of the present day is the culmination of a process that has been going on for millennia, despite many interruptions and setbacks. The dispersion of humankind over the habitable continents is believed to have taken some 50,000 years from when our ancestors first ventured on foot out of Africa. Adapting to an extreme range of conditions by cultural innovations rather than biological diversification, we remained a single species. Beginning around the end of the last glacial period, the centrifugal tendency was reversed. Branches of the human family, long oblivious of each other's existence, were slowly relinked through migrations, trade, conquests and religion. Technological developments made distance less and less of an obstacle to contact and mutual influence. For better or worse, our lives have become increasingly interconnected.[3]

Whether we welcome this interconnectedness or not, it has become impossible to ignore it. Meanwhile not only our relationship with the rest of humanity, but our perception of the earth itself has changed. This, too, has happened gradually over centuries, but has accelerated significantly in the past few decades. Photographs of the earth as seen from outer space have heightened our awareness of the planet. The Gaia Theory has made it possible to speak scientifically of the earth as a living system. There are growing concerns about the impact of industrial civilization on the balance of this system.

Knowledge of the spherical shape of the earth began to have an impact on the course of history by the late fifteenth century, when Europeans tried to reach the "East" by sailing west and discovered, instead, a continent hitherto unknown

---

2 Steger 2003: 12.

3 See Chanda 2007.

to them. But the notion that the earth is round was not new, nor was it confined to Europe. In Greece it can be traced to Pythagoras in the sixth century BCE. In India it is perhaps even older. *Aitareya Brāhmaṇa* states that the sun never sets, nor does it rise,[4] suggesting that our impression of the sun's daily motion is due to the rotation of the earth.

The earth's circumference was estimated by Eratosthenes of Alexandria in the third century BCE. The Indian mathematician and astronomer Āryabhaṭa arrived at a more accurate calculation in the fifth century CE. Works by Āryabhaṭa and other Indian scientists were later translated into Arabic and from Arabic into Latin. Thus some knowledge of Indian science and mathematics reached medieval Europe through the Muslims, who also passed on the legacy of Greek science and made contributions of their own. The dissemination of Chinese inventions, including printing, was another factor leading to the scientific revolution and our present view of the world we live in.[5] That revolution could not have occurred without the kind of cultural transmissions we now associate with globalization. More than we think, such transmissions were taking place constantly, though at a slower pace than today, even between premodern civilizations.

Columbus and the Riches of India

According to a popular myth, in the Middle Ages people believed the earth to be flat. This fable was invented in the

4 *sa vā eṣa na kadācanāstameti nodeti* (*Aitareya Brāhmaṇa* 3.44) (Haug 1863, vol. 1: 81; vol. 2: 242). The dating of the Brāhmaṇas is conjectural; they are commonly assigned to the seventh and eighth centuries BCE or thereabouts.

5 Arun Bala (2006) critiques the Eurocentric belief that no scientific tradition except that of the Greeks, passively transmitted by the Arabs, played an important role in the emergence of modern science.

nineteenth century to dramatize the supposed contrast between medieval ignorance and modern enlightenment. What is true is that up to the time of Columbus the shape and size of the earth were matters of mainly theoretical interest. With Columbus the concept of the globe became an idea that would change the world. Yet Christopher Columbus, the self-educated son of an Italian weaver, made history not because he knew what he was doing, but because he managed to make his rash proposal look profitable to the rulers who financed it. In fact, he wildly underestimated the distance to Asia, though better figures were readily available. He and the crew of his three ships would have perished in mid-ocean, never to be heard of again, if they had not chanced upon an unsuspected continent that lay across their route.

The oldest surviving spherical map of the earth was made in 1492, the year of Columbus's first voyage. This globe known as the Erdapfel (earth apple) was built by Martin Behaim, a German navigator employed by the king of Portugal. It shows only a narrow ocean between Europe and Asia. Asia appears on the map as Marco Polo described it, with Japan 1,500 miles offshore. Columbus drew his information from the same sources as Behaim and hoped that such an easily navigable ocean would give him access to the riches of India.[6] With this fanciful picture of the earth in mind he persuaded his royal patrons to ignore expert opinions and fund his reckless adventure. The age of European expansion over both the hemispheres had begun.

The idea of the globe, however inaccurately conceived, was starting to take hold of the European mind. Vast uncharted spaces called for exploration. Portugal took the lead until Spain entered the contest by sponsoring Columbus. Thirty years after Columbus's first voyage, the circumnavigation of

6 Fernández-Armesto 2000: 27.

the globe was achieved by the handful of Magellan's crew who survived the three-year expedition. Europeans were beginning to think of the earth as a whole. Unfortunately for non-Europeans, they looked at it mainly as land, resources and people to be possessed, exploited and subjected. Gold, slaves and colonies would be among their principal objects of pursuit in the coming centuries.

The West and the Rest

The upshot of it all was a world dominated politically, economically and culturally by the West. Globalization as we know it has been the outcome of this one-sided process. But many students of the past and observers of the present now regard the rise of the West as a passing phase. The economist Clyde Prestowitz, for instance, distinguishes three waves of globalization: the wave of European expansion and imperialism from around 1415 to 1914, which collapsed in the period of the two world wars and the Great Depression; a wave of American-led globalization from 1947 to 2000; and a third wave, just begun, which he thinks is likely to shift wealth and power back to Asia. He sums up the situation at the outset of the first wave:

> In 1415 China and the area we now call India produced about 75 percent of the global GDP. America was still undiscovered, and the countries of Europe were insignificant and backward. They were aware of the wealth of the East only because Arabs who controlled the overland trade routes deigned from time to time to let a few scraps fall from the table to the Western "infidel" dogs.[7]

In the five centuries after 1415, of course, all this was to be reversed with a vengeance. It began with Europeans finding sea routes to bypass the Arabs and lay their own hands on the riches of the East. This daring move revealed a spirit of

---

[7] Prestowitz 2005: 8.

adventure and a willingness to take risks. But the West's conquest of the globe also depended on more dubious qualities which belied the claims of moral superiority often put forward at the time to justify European supremacy.

1492 was an ominous year in this regard. In Spain, it was a year of the triumph of religious intolerance. The completion of the Reconquista with the fall of Granada paved the way for ridding Iberia of the Muslims who had played an important part in its culture for several centuries. This was followed shortly by the Alhambra Decree, or "Edict of Expulsion". Tens of thousands of Jews who refused to convert to Christianity were forced to flee either to Portugal, where they escaped persecution for only a few years, or to the more welcoming arms of the Ottoman Empire.

Meanwhile Columbus had stumbled upon the "New World", with disastrous consequences for the indigenous peoples of the Western Hemisphere. There, 1492 marked the beginning of what has been described as the American Holocaust.[8] The conquistadors and settlers failed to recognize that the populations being decimated were those of their long-lost brothers and sisters, another branch of the human family which had separated from their own many thousands of years ago.

Globalization, in so far as it is a product of Western expansionism, can be said to have begun with the Portuguese explorations in the fifteenth century and the joining of the hemispheres through Columbus's voyages. But long before Europe emerged from its Dark Ages, the human race was being slowly drawn together through exchanges that were not dominated by any one civilization. Peaceful transmissions such as the spread of Buddhism from India to China in the first millennium CE suggest that interactions among people of

---

[8] Stannard 1992.

different cultures need not always be to the advantage of some and to the detriment of others.

Even the impact of the modern West upon the rest of the world, for all the exploitation and violence that accompanied it, has not been an unmitigated evil. Few would wish to undo all the changes that have occurred in human life in the last few centuries. The West has all too often shown its worst side in its dealings with the non-Western world. But there has been more to the West than the fanaticism, brutality and greed of crusaders, conquistadors and colonialists. Its positive side can be seen even if we focus on the otherwise inauspicious year 1492 and the period around it, when the transition from the medieval to the modern age was under way.

The Spirit of the Renaissance

In the late fifteenth century, the Renaissance reached its peak in Italy and began to spread to the rest of Europe. The rediscovery of ancient Greek and Roman civilization stimulated a revival of the free activity of the mind which had been restricted by medieval Christianity. The most versatile genius of the age was Leonardo da Vinci. In his *Vitruvian Man*, drawn in or around 1492, he captured the spirit of Renaissance humanism. This outlook on human nature was to play a decisive role in the later development of European culture. With the spread of Western influence, it would affect to some degree every culture on earth.

Vitruvian Man is on one level a study of proportion. The ancient Roman architect Vitruvius regarded the human body as a natural temple whose perfect proportions provide a model for architecture to follow. Inspired by Vitruvius's observations on the relationship of the body to geometrical shapes, Leonardo drew a human figure with the arms and legs in two superimposed positions so that the hands and feet touch both a square and a circle.

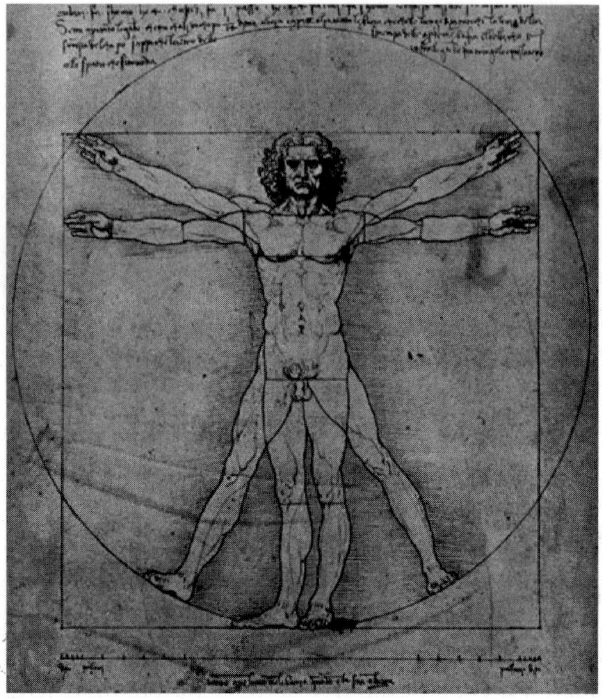

But *Vitruvian Man* is more than a technical study. Breaking medieval taboos by his revival of the classical nude, Leonardo was able to combine anatomical realism with geometrical symbolism conveying an idealistic vision of humanity's place in the scheme of things.

Earlier in the fifteenth century, Nicholas of Cusa had used the square and the circle to illustrate his Neoplatonic conception of man as the point in the universe where the finite and the infinite meet. The square stands for the finite; the circle represents infinity, for it corresponds to a polygon with the number of angles indefinitely multiplied.[9] Leonardo was almost certainly aware of the Cardinal of Cusa's ideas. Interpreting *Vitruvian Man* in this light, art historian Martin Germ explains:

---

[9] Bellitto, Izbicki and Christianson 2004: 9, 386.

> Man is subject to all limitations of the world (therefore inscribed in a square), but the inexhaustible power of his creative spirit in motion (indicated through the circular motion of the human body forming the circle) simultaneously lifts him above those limitations.[10]

Vitruvian Man, drawn over 500 years ago, is one of the most frequently reproduced artistic images in the world today. It evokes a vision of the human potential that is a distinctive contribution of the West to the emerging global culture. However, Western civilization has not been altogether faithful to this Renaissance vision of balance between the physical existence and the higher faculties. Materialism has tended to imprison our consciousness, as it were, in the square of Leonardo's drawing. And materialism has now been globalized into a worldwide malady.

The Expanding Universe

Soon after Leonardo drew *Vitruvian Man*, he constructed one of the earliest known terrestrial globes after Behaim's. The idea of the globe was in the air and would continue to grow. A century after Leonardo da Vinci, William Shakespeare was writing plays for the Globe Theatre and taking as his subject nothing less than "the great globe itself, / Yea, all which it inherit".[11]

These lines in *The Tempest* were written around 1610. In the same year, Galileo Galilei published the first astronomical observations made with a telescope. These seemed to support the heliocentric model of the solar system proposed by Nicolaus Copernicus early in the preceding century. The telescope also showed the universe to be much larger than was previously supposed. Meanwhile Johannes Kepler had published his first two laws of planetary motion, solving some

---

[10] Germ 2007: 105.

[11] William Shakespeare, *The Tempest*, Act 4, Scene 1.

of the technical problems that still plagued the Copernican theory. A revolution in the perception of the "great globe" and its place in the cosmos was under way.

Late in his life, Galileo claimed that "by marvellous discoveries and clear demonstrations" he had enlarged the universe "a hundred thousand times beyond the belief of the wise men of bygone ages". As the Buddhist scholar Edward Conze has pointed out,

> Europeans in the 17th century were quite unaware that *"the wise men of bygone ages"* in India had for a long time already done justice to the immensity of time and space, not, however, through *marvellous discoveries and clear demonstrations,* but through the intuitions of their cosmic imagination.[12]

This grandiose cosmic imagination was alien, for the most part, to the Western world-view up to Galileo's time. The resistance he encountered culminated in a dramatic confrontation with the Church. Yet the Catholic Church had not initially forbidden astronomers to consider Copernicus's hypothesis. When Giordano Bruno was burned at the stake in 1600, it was for theological heresies rather than his heliocentric views that he was condemned. But the Protestant Reformation had put the Church on the defensive and Galileo's headstrong temperament made matters worse. His *Dialogue Concerning the Two Chief World Systems* was published in 1632 with papal permission, but by strongly advocating his own position he broke an agreement that he would present both sides of the issue evenhandedly. Losing the Pope's support, he was called before the Inquisition and forced to recant.

Religious conservatism and institutional power had prevailed for the moment over empirical inquiry and individual genius. But it was a Pyrrhic victory for the Church which undermined its authority in the long run. By the end of

---

12 Conze 1959: 49; Galileo's phrases italicized by Conze.

the century, Isaac Newton had consolidated the foundations of Copernican cosmology in an elegant and imposing synthesis of the work of his predecessors. Men like Bernard le Bovier de Fontenelle, perhaps the first successful writer of popular science, brought the changed picture of the world before the general public. Fontenelle's *Conversations on the Plurality of Worlds* was published in French in 1686, a year before Newton's *Principia*. In it a philosopher explains the new astronomy to a lady as they walk in a garden at night gazing at the stars. She responds with dismay:

> The universe is so big that I am lost in it, I don't know where I am any more; I have become nothing. The earth is so terribly small![13]

Blaise Pascal, too, had been appalled by "the eternal silence of these infinite spaces".[14] As the notion of a drastically expanded cosmos and a comparatively diminutive earth became more familiar, thoughtful minds reacted in various ways. For Voltaire it heightened the absurdity of religious intolerance, drawing from him the exclamation:

> O God, our common father, God of mercy, make it possible that on our little globe, on this, the least of Thy worlds, there be neither fanatics nor persecutors.[15]

In the late twentieth century, the astronomer Carl Sagan echoed this sentiment. Reflecting on the photograph of the earth called the Pale Blue Dot, taken by the Voyager 1 spacecraft in 1990 from a distance of four billion miles, he wrote:

> Look again at that dot. That's here. That's home. That's us. On it everyone you love, everyone you know, everyone you

[13] Quoted in French by Bury (1955: 115); my translation.

[14] Pascal 2005: 64.

[15] Peters 1989: 181.

> ever heard of, every human being who ever was, lived out their lives. . . . Think of the endless cruelties visited by the inhabitants of one corner of this pixel on the scarcely distinguishable inhabitants of some other corner. . . . To me, it underscores our responsibility to deal more kindly with one another, and to preserve and cherish the pale blue dot, the only home we've ever known.[16]

Breaking Down Barriers

Small as the earth now seemed when compared with the vastness of the universe, it was still large enough for all practical purposes. Most people shrugged their shoulders at the revelations of the astronomers and went about their daily business. Even so, they could hardly fail to notice the changes taking place all around them. Scientific discoveries not only altered how the world was perceived, but led to technological innovations with more tangible consequences. The Scientific Revolution was followed by the Industrial Revolution. It all fostered the growth of the concept that defined the modern age: the idea of progress.

By the late nineteenth century, Europeans and Americans could look back at the preceding few hundred years and marvel at how far their societies had advanced. The earth was now "shrinking" ever more rapidly; it took less and less time and effort to travel to or communicate with distant lands. Some cultural developments were no less striking. Religion seemed to have shed its worst excesses: heretics and witches were no longer burned. Biblical literalism, already shaken by Copernicus, was given a further blow by Darwin. God was pronounced dead. But this was surely premature. Even in the West, religion whether conservative or liberal was far from being a spent force. Though fundamentalism was not yet christened, the reactions to cultural and theological modernism

---

16 Sagan 1997: 6-7.

that would soon take this name were already gathering momentum. Yet religion could still play a progressive role. It could not only divide humanity, but bring it together.

A watershed event in religious history occurred in Chicago as part of the World's Columbian Exposition. Like other world's fairs since the Great Exhibition in London in 1851, the Exposition was a celebration of Western expansion, scientific and industrial progress, and what we would now call economic globalization. But globalization was also breaking down cultural barriers. Nothing showed this more clearly than the Parliament of Religions.

The Parliament translated the Exposition's triumphalism into religious terms. "Who can tell," wrote a certain Bishop Whitehead of Pittsburg, "but that the great Head of the Church may, in his providence, make use of this immense gathering to usher in the triumph of his truth, when at the name of Jesus every knee shall bow?"[17] But whatever the motives of its organizers and supporters, the stage was set for a historic encounter between East and West whose course no one could foresee or control.

For more than two weeks in September 1893, thousands of people listened to speakers from all over the world representing a variety of cultures and most of the major religions. The Asian delegates made an impact far out of proportion to their relatively small numbers. Extensive newspaper coverage made possible such a phenomenon as the sudden fame of Swami Vivekananda. He had arrived from India unknown and uninvited and was turned away when he first presented himself in Chicago. In the end he was allowed to speak in the name of Hinduism. Overnight he found himself to be one of the Parliament's most acclaimed personalities and was soon launched on a whirlwind lecture tour.

---

[17] Barrows 1893, vol. 1: 24-25.

News of America's open-armed reception of Vivekananda sent a thrill through the masses of India. The first stirrings of a national resurgence were felt in what is today the world's largest democracy, then an impoverished population demoralized by the indignities of foreign rule. When Vivekananda appeared on the platform in Chicago, India strode onto the stage of the modern world. Soon "the awakening of the torpid Colossus began",[18] as the French Nobel laureate Romain Rolland wrote with reference to the impact of Vivekananda's speeches on the huge crowds that greeted him when he, who had left his country as an unknown ascetic, returned to it as a national hero.

Within a few decades, the colonial era had faded into history. To be sure, American hegemony promptly replaced European imperialism. Not only modernization but Westernization seemed for a while to be continuing unabated. But today there is little reason to doubt that revitalized Asian and other nations, however they may evolve through the interactions of a globalized world, will preserve the continuity of their basic cultural identities.

The course that globalization is likely to take in the future is a subject of lively debate. As the expansionism of the modern West collides with the finitude of the earth and the revival of non-Western cultures, some scholars expect to see a radical change of direction – in the words of the sociologist Martin Albrow, the "final reversal of the process begun by Columbus".[19] From a Western perspective, as Albrow points out, exchange with

> rival civilizations, such as India and China, which operated in different conceptual frames in totally different configurations . . . is now a factor in the transformation which makes the Global Age. For they proved resilient and

18 Rolland 2004: 93.

19 Albrow 1996: 100. Albrow refers to Sachs 1993: 20.

> capable of resisting Western domination and their survival highlights the limits of modernity.[20]

In any case, only a worldwide catastrophe – unfortunately by no means inconceivable – could undo the fundamental change in humanity's collective life brought about by the developments of recent history. By the early twentieth century, the Indian philosopher Sri Aurobindo could speak of "a newly created, though still loose, natural organic unity of mankind, . . . a closely interdependent existence of the constituent parts in which the life and movements of one affect the life of the others in a way which would have been impossible a hundred years ago". Elaborating on the nature of this interdependence, soon to be dubbed globalization, he continued:

> Continent has no longer a separate life from continent; no nation can any longer isolate itself at will and live a separate existence. Science, commerce and rapid communications have produced a state of things in which the disparate masses of humanity, once living to themselves, have been drawn together by a process of subtle unification into a single mass which has already a common vital and is rapidly forming a common mental existence.[21]

Among the challenges we face in this ever more interconnected world, there are two whose urgency stands out. Our national and international life must be reshaped so that the affluence of some no longer depends on or coexists with the poverty of others. And we need to form a new, sustainable relationship with "this little whirling globe",[22] smaller and frailer than we once imagined, which carries us all on our enigmatic journey through the immensities of space and time.

---

20 Albrow 1996: 35.

21 Aurobindo 1998b: 193. The chapter containing the quoted passages was first published in June 1917.

22 Aurobindo 1993: 330.

2

An Unmanageable Encounter
The Meeting of Religions and Cultures in Chicago, 1893

> *We are becoming aware that the "orientalization of the world" . . . is a distinct global process – although the task of unpacking the range of cultural associations summoned up by this concept, and their place in the continuing struggles to define the global cultural order, has yet to begin.*
>
> – Mike Featherstone 1990: 12

The World's Parliament of Religions in History

On the morning of 11 September 1893, with fanfare and pageantry, the world's first Parliament of Religions opened in Chicago. The seventeen-day event, held in conjunction with the mammoth World's Columbian Exposition, was the brainchild of Charles Carroll Bonney, a Swedenborgian lawyer and comparative religions enthusiast.[1] As chairman of the

[1] The eighteenth-century Swedish mystic Emanuel Swedenborg was highly esteemed by the religious avant-garde in nineteenth-century America. Charles Bonney's Swedenborgianism is important, therefore, for understanding one aspect of the Parliament. Religious historian Catherine Albanese observes: "Something akin to the immanential theology of Swedenborg . . . ran through the organizing ideology of the entire World's Parliament event" (2007: 333). But the part played by Bonney and thus by Swedenborg in shaping this ideology was offset, as we will see, by the more conservative role of John Henry Barrows.

World's Congress Auxiliary, which organized some twenty congresses on various topics during the summer of 1893, Bonney considered the religious congress to be the culmination of the Exposition. Welcoming the assembly, he declared that it was convened in the hope of "marking the actual beginning of a new epoch of brotherhood and peace".[2] His optimism was echoed in subsequent speeches. The anticipation of great things to come was heightened by the colorful presence, on the platform, of speakers from far corners of the earth. There was a sense that history had reached a momentous turning point.

The century or so that followed sadly belied the expectations aroused by the Parliament. The anniversary of its inauguration, September 11 itself, now has dramatically different associations. Yet in a number of ways this unprecedented gathering in the late nineteenth century, bringing participants from diverse religions and cultures face to face, did point toward a "new epoch". It did not usher in peace or unity, though it initiated a movement of interfaith dialogue. But perhaps more importantly, at the height of the colonial era it provided a forum where the discourse of Western exceptionalism, the assertion of the superiority of values derived from European civilization, could be publicly challenged by representatives of non-Western cultures.

It matters little that the forum was officially apolitical. Issues pertaining to the global balance of power were just below the surface. In the mid-twentieth century, the transition to an age of more equal relations among civilizations would begin with decolonization. Well in advance, its advent was symbolically foreshadowed at the extraordinary confluence of human diversity in Chicago. If the Parliament is worth talking about today, it is partly because it was a spectacular

[2] Barrows 1893, vol. 1: 67. Bonney's speech is reprinted in Seager and Kidd 1993: 17-22.

failure for the dream of Christian inclusivism that inspired many of its organizers and supporters. Its failure to achieve its proclaimed objectives is the key to its enduring significance.

What is most remarkable about the Parliament of Religions is the degree to which the issues it raised over 100 years ago are relevant to our own times. In this age of globalization, multiculturalism and religious resurgence, the same issues confront us in new forms in our post-Cold War and post-9/11 world. Some historians have minimized the Parliament's tangible influence and consequences. Yet an event that in many ways was so far ahead of its time may deserve more attention than its actual achievements seem to justify. Several features of the Parliament invite us to look at it in the largest possible context. The more we do so, the more it repays our study.

A Global Cultural Event

Globalization is the broadest and most basic context for situating the Parliament of Religions in history. Such an event could hardly have been conceived much earlier in the process of growing interconnectedness whose latest developments we usually have in mind when we now speak of globalization. The word "globalization" itself did not enter into the common lexicon until the 1960s. By the 1980s it was becoming both a subject of extensive academic study and a popular buzzword. But in the view of some scholars, globalization was already well under way between around 1890 and 1914, during the later part of the *belle époque* (or, in America, the Gilded Age). In terms of certain factors such as the openness of national economies to trade and the scale of migration, they even argue that the world today is less globalized than it was then.

Economically, the integration of world markets became possible in the second half of the nineteenth century with the advent of telegraph. As sociologist Paul Hirst and political economist Grahame Thompson point out,

> If the theorists of globalization mean that we have an economy in which each part of the world is linked by markets sharing close to real-time information, then that began not in the 1970s but in the 1870s.[3]

Politically, the international system is more fragmented by national borders in the early twenty-first century than it was in the age of imperialism.

The cultural dimension of globalization is the aspect of it most directly related to our topic. The Parliament of Religions was among the first instances of a global cultural event. Its repercussions in distant lands were largely due to the rapid growth of mass circulation newspapers since the 1830s. Sociologist Anthony Giddens notes the "globalizing impact of media" by the last decade of the nineteenth century:

> Thus one commentator in 1892 wrote that, as a result of modern newspapers, the inhabitant of a local village has a broader understanding of contemporary events than the prime minister of a hundred years before. The villager who reads a paper "interests himself simultaneously in the issue of a revolution in Chile, a bush-war in East Africa, a massacre in North China, a famine in Russia".[4]

This awareness of worldwide events put the discussion of religion in a new perspective. At the Parliament, a certain William Alger reminded the audience that Hindus and Muslims had just been fighting each other in far-away Bombay, while clashes between Catholics and Protestants were occurring in nearby Montreal and Toronto.[5] His address on "How to Achieve Religious Unity" was thus placed in a global as well as historical context that would not have been so readily available a few decades earlier.

---

[3] Held and McGrew 2003: 101.

[4] Giddens 2003: 65. Giddens quotes from Nordau 1892/1968: 39.

[5] Marty 1997: 20.

We need not hesitate, then, to speak of globalization in the late nineteenth century. Some scholars extend the historical timeframe of globalization even further back. They maintain that its present forms are the continuation and intensification of processes that began some five centuries ago with the emergence of modernity and the capitalist world-system. Still another view – the least Eurocentric – is that economic, political and cultural processes that can only be described as globalizing have been going on for thousands of years.

Whatever our theory of globalization, a decisive phase in the long march of history was the period of Western expansion, beginning in the fifteenth century, which among other things led to the flooding of the so-called New World with colonists from Europe. The results of this expansionism were explicitly celebrated in the World's Columbian Exposition in Chicago. The Parliament of Religions was conceived largely in the same spirit, but took an unexpected turn and earned a place in history for quite different reasons.

From Columbus to Vivekananda

The Exposition ran from May to October 1893. In those six months it drew some 27 million people, equivalent then to roughly half the population of the United States. This number dwarfs the audience of 4,000 that could be packed at any one time into the newly-built Hall of Columbus where the main sessions of the Parliament of Religions were held.[6] But the Parliament, with its exalted aspirations, shared the grandiosity of the Exposition. At times it even surpassed it in high-flown rhetoric, compounding the Exposition's American triumphalism with Christian millennialism.

---

[6] The figure of 7,000 which is sometimes cited includes the capacity of the adjoining Hall of Washington, where supplementary sessions were held and on some days the main program was repeated for an overflow crowd. See Barrows 1893, vol. 1: 157-58 and Burke 1992, vol. 1: 74-75, 79.

Both the Columbian Exposition and the Hall of Columbus were so named in honor of the Italian explorer, employed by the monarchs of Spain, whose voyage in 1492 was credited with linking the Old World with the New. The Exposition was meant to be held in 1892 to celebrate the four hundredth anniversary of that epochal event. The scale of the preparations, involving the construction of an entire town called the White City, delayed it by a year. But in the light of recent scholarship, it seems not inappropriate that the commemoration of Columbus's discovery took place in 1893. Clarifying the precise nature of Columbus's accomplishment, the historian Felipe Fernández-Armesto points out the importance of 1493 in this connection:

> What Columbus discovered was a route from Europe to the New World and back which was previously unrecorded and which remained, with some modifications, the standard route throughout the age of sail. Strictly speaking, this was an achievement of 1493, not 1492, since Columbus's first outward route proved unsatisfactory and it was only on his second crossing that he made the best possible use of the Atlantic wind-system. World history is a matter of cultural transmissions at long range, which depend on explorers for route-finding. Columbus found routes which, for the first time and forever, established viable, commercially exploitable and durable links between hemispheres which then began to influence each other in re-shaping ways.[7]

Fernández-Armesto's last phrase suggests a parallel of sorts between Columbus's achievement of 1493 and the outcome of the assembly convened 400 years later in the hall named after him. The Parliament of Religions likewise established, though in a different sense, "durable links between hemispheres which then began to influence each other in re-shaping ways". For better or worse, Columbus's voyages in 1492-93 marked the

7 Fernández-Armesto 2000: xiii.

European arrival in the Americas. In 1893 the Asians who surprised the world at the Parliament arrived as bearers of Eastern philosophy and spirituality on the same shores, by then populated mostly by immigrants from Europe. To this day, the consequences of this new and more benign linking of the hemispheres continue to unfold.

In the last century, the tide of Western power and influence that was rising since Columbus has begun to recede. The Parliament's quest for the unity of religions on a Christian foundation was the religious manifestation of a mindset created by 400 years of expansion. The frustration of this attempt to put forward the vision of a Christianized world gave a foretaste of the faltering of the expansionist impulse of Western civilization in the decades to come.

Swami Vivekananda, the uninvited guest from India who memorably crashed the party in Chicago, had little patience with Christian pretensions to superiority. Nevertheless, he appreciated the cosmopolitanism of the Parliament. He praised his hosts for their "great attempt . . . to break down the barriers of this little world of ours".[8] But the real breaking of barriers occurred because things did not go according to plan. Though the appearance of a Christian victory was kept up in the end, the unanticipated impact of the Asian visitors was no secret. The principal historian of the Parliament, Richard Seager, observes:

> Given the momentum of Western expansion, the tenor of the Columbiad, and the skewed playing field of the Parliament, the Asian delegates entered the contest between East and West as underdogs, but these charismatic individuals emerged from the theological fracas on the floor as darkhorse candidates.[9]

---

[8] Vivekananda 1989, vol. 1: 5.

[9] Seager 1995: 108-09.

This drama was what caught the attention of the general public. Even today, the Parliament is worth remembering for this surprise turn of events, not for its thwarted aspiration to win universal acceptance for a religious discourse dominated by the West and centered around Jesus Christ.

Human Brotherhood and the "Problem of Heathenism"

In the long run, the Parliament contributed to the growth of more equal and mutually respectful interactions between Eastern and Western religions and cultures. This had begun before 1893, but has greatly accelerated since then. The one-sided influence of the West on the East in the preceding period has been partially reversed by Eastern ideas infiltrating the West. The equality and reciprocity of religions and cultures are not exactly what most of the organizers of the Parliament wanted to bring about, however. For all their rhetoric of brotherhood, part of their motive was to reinforce the triumphalism of the Columbian extravaganza with a religious sanction giving it a halo of Christian universality.

In the 1890s, imperialism was in the air. America was not immune to it, nor were religious leaders necessarily less hawkish than politicians. Josiah Strong was a Protestant clergyman and one of the founders of the Social Gospel, usually considered a liberal movement. In 1893 he published *The New Era*, where he asked:

> Is it not reasonable to believe that this race is destined to dispossess many weaker ones, assimilate others, and mould the remainder, until, in a very true and important sense, it has Anglo-Saxonized mankind?[10]

Catholic historian Gary Wills comments:

---

[10] Strong 1893: 79-80.

> condemning, this action of the General Assembly produced very little effect.[15]

Actually, the vote condemning the Parliament reflected deeper problems in the church than Barrows was willing to admit. It was an early symptom of a division that would continue until the fundamentalist–modernist controversy in American Presbyterianism came to a head in the 1920s and 1930s and led to a schism. Similar schisms occurred in other denominations.

A "Many-colored Bubble"

The meeting of East and West in Chicago took place against the background of America's own culture wars. The successes and failures of the Parliament of Religions can only be understood in this context. Its numerous opponents saw it as furthering the agenda of liberals and radicals. To conservative Christians, the Parliament was an act of aggression against traditional values. They reacted accordingly. Dwight Moody, for example, would have nothing to do with it. Moody is sometimes called the father of American fundamentalism, though he died in 1899 before the word "fundamentalism" was coined. It was probably fortunate that he and others of a similar persuasion chose to ignore an event that was contentious enough without them.

Moody's refusal to participate was recounted by an associate of his, a certain Rev. H.M. Wharton, who added comments of his own which many contemporaries would have agreed with:

> When this ecclesiastical menagerie, gathered from all quarters of the globe, made its appearance, Mr. Moody was asked again and again to take part. He only replied that he had his hands full of work, and declined to go. When it seemed to some of us that our Lord was belittled and

---

15 Barrows 1893, vol. 1: 19.

> disgraced by the motley crew who disported themselves upon the platform day by day in the wonderful "Parliament", we suggested that we should attack them all along the line. Mr. Moody was very emphatic in his instructions. "Preach Christ," said he, "hold up Christ; let the Parliament of Religions alone, preach Christ." And he was right. The many-colored bubble burst, and went to thin air. It will hardly be known in history. Christ lives and reigns; let us live for Him and preach His blessed Gospel.[16]

The Parliament of Religions has been called the dawn of religious pluralism.[17] But in America in the 1890s, religious pluralism as we now understand it was a radical idea with little support in the social reality of the time. It would be decades before this changed. Few of the organizers of the Parliament had any conception of what we would now recognize as pluralism. Theologically speaking, the major issue in American religion was the quarrel between exclusivism and inclusivism. This corresponded more or less to the social divide between conservatives and liberals. The voluntary self-exclusion of the exclusivists/conservatives from the Parliament made it a liberal forum. It could have been a rather uneventful occasion if the orientals had played their part according to the script. Because they did not, the Parliament ended up anticipating some of the issues proper to the very different and more complex social reality we confront today.

---

16 Chapman 1900: chapter 33, "Personal Reminiscences of D.L. Moody," accessed 21 April 2014, http://www.biblebelievers.com/moody/33.html.

17 In the foreword to *The Dawn of Religious Pluralism*, Diana Eck accepts with some caveats the evaluation of the Parliament's significance implied by the title of the volume. While it "captures the vision of the Parliament", she points out, "we must be somewhat cautious in acquiescing to its claims. . . . For some, this was surely the dawn of what we might call pluralism. . . . For others, however, this plurality was seen as but a step on the way to an emerging world religion." (Seager and Kidd 1993: xiii-xiv.)

> and orange was hardly less interesting than these earnest words and the rich, rhythmical utterance he gave them.[28]

As this statement suggests, the audience was not concerned only with theological issues. Vivekananda and some other Asian speakers were as philosophically sophisticated as anyone on the platform, but it was not only by reasoning that they swayed their hearers. The reference to the Hallelujah chorus shows how the effectiveness of the Christian discourse depended on stirring the emotions. The comparative handful of Asians were handicapped in a number of ways as they tried to present an alternative discourse. But they quickly discovered their own advantages and put them to good use.

Seager points out that

> leading Asians at the Parliament held a position that gave them a strategic leverage; they were of the East, and thus untainted by the West, yet able to utilize modern and western concepts, values and sentiments to serve their own ends.[29]

Most of the Asian participants came from cultures that had begun to evolve a critical and creative response to the European impact, absorbing much but adapting it to their own needs. Even as they accepted modernity, they dissociated it as far as possible from its Western origins and made it their own. The modernity of these Asians allowed them to participate successfully in a global forum. But it was as representatives of an emerging *Asian* modernity that they made their debut on the world stage.

The Exotic Cosmopolitan

The thirty-year-old Vivekananda and two or three others – notably the even younger Dharmapala from what was then

---

28 Burke 1992, vol. 1: 137.

29 Seager 1995: 96.

Ceylon – stood out among these brilliant young men from the East. A combination of cosmopolitanism and exoticism contributed to Swami Vivekananda's exceptional ability to bond with his Western audiences, both in Chicago and on subsequent tours. He was fascinatingly different, yet he spoke their language and by all accounts spoke it superbly. He had assimilated Western thought and, at the same time, fathomed the depths of his own tradition. But he kept his independence and creatively remolded his tradition for modern conditions. For all his love of India, he was a planetary citizen.

When Vivekananda was returning to India after his first visit to the West, as his ship neared Port Said he wrote:

> From Suez begins Asia. Once more Asia. What am I? Asiatic, European, or American? I feel a curious medley of personalities in me.[30]

This hybrid identity enabled him to bridge cultures and represent India in a way that the West could understand. He was a breaker of barriers, contemptuous of narrow and exclusive identities. In this respect Vivekananda's achievement was consistent with what he appreciated in the quest for unity at the Parliament of Religions. Yet he saw the disguised imperialism implicit in much of the talk of brotherhood. He was an unsparing critic of Christian ambitions for global religious hegemony.

The Asian presence at the Parliament was not the one-man show that Swami Vivekananda's admirers sometimes imagine. It is true, though, that the delegates from the Far East were overshadowed by the South Asians, among whom Vivekananda became perhaps the most famous. This was partly due to unintended consequences of British colonialism. We can only guess how effective the substantial Japanese contingent

---

30 Vivekananda 1989, vol. 8: 395.

3

Civilizations and Post-Cold War Conflict

> *"Colonialism" may have triumphed in the past; but today it is an obvious fiasco. And colonialism, typically, is the submergence of one civilization by another. The conquered always submit to the stronger; but their submission is merely provisional when civilizations clash.*
>
> – Fernand Braudel 1993: 33

Huntington and His Critics

In 1993 Samuel Huntington wrote in the influential American journal *Foreign Affairs*:

> With the end of the Cold War, international politics moves out of its Western phase, and its centerpiece becomes the interaction between the West and non-Western civilizations and among non-Western civilizations. In the politics of civilizations, the peoples and governments of non-Western civilizations no longer remain the objects of history as targets of Western colonialism but join the West as movers and shapers of history.[1]

This was a momentous insight. Both the article entitled "The Clash of Civilizations?" and the subsequent book, *The Clash of Civilizations and the Remaking of World Order*, generated a good deal of discussion. But the alarmism of the "clash of civilizations" thesis distracted attention from Huntington's

[1] Huntington 2000: 4.

constructive reflections on a multicivilizational world order. Contrary to his reputation as a hawk, he warned the United States against intervening in the affairs of countries belonging to other civilizations. He advocated a reform of the United Nations Security Council to include permanent seats for Japan, India and representatives of Africa, Latin America and the Muslim world. More generally, he recommended that

> peoples in all civilizations should search for and attempt to expand the values, institutions, and practices they have in common with peoples of other civilizations.[2]

Huntington has had many critics. He has also been frequently misunderstood. One of the more substantial critiques is that of the international relations theorist John Hobson. Like many others, however, Hobson distorts Huntington's position. In *The Eurocentric Conception of World Politics*, he contrasts Huntington's anti-imperialist "defensive Eurocentrism" with the neo-imperialist "paternalist Eurocentrism" of most liberal international theory. There is some justification for treating Huntington's anti-imperialism as a variant of Western international theory's pervasive Eurocentrism, though tempered in his case by a recognition that the West is no longer in charge of things. But Hobson misreads Huntington when he quotes as "one of the clearest signs" of his Eurocentric approach some sentences from the last two paragraphs of *The Clash of Civilizations*, beginning:

> On a worldwide basis Civilization seems in many respects to be yielding to barbarism. . . .[3]

Hobson thinks this passage proves his contention that Huntington feared the "barbaric threat" that the Chinese and Muslims, especially, pose for Western civilization.[4] But

---

2 Huntington 1997: 312, 317-18, 320.

3 Hobson 2012: 284.

4 Ibid.: 279.

> Without such intellectual constructs, there is, as William James said, only "a bloomin' buzzin' confusion".[7]

The question, of course, is whether the things Huntington's map omits, distorts or obscures are sufficiently outweighed by the advantages of conceptual clarity it offers. Many scholars in a variety of fields do not think so. Political philosopher Martha Nussbaum, for example, remarks:

> When we are dealing with a complex and variegated world, the simplistic notion of a "clash of civilizations" is not helpful.

Thinking in such terms, according to her,

> leads us to ignore both the heterogeneity of all known civilizations and the interpenetration and mutual influence among cultures that is a fact of human history.[8]

Sociologist Jan Nederveen Pieterse is scathing:

> Huntington's position stands out for its blatant admixture of security interests and a crude rendition of civilizational difference.

He continues along the same lines as Hobson:

> In view of its demagogic character it obviously belongs to the genre of "new enemy" discourse. In fact, it merges two existing enemy discourses, the "fundamentalist threat" of Islam and the "yellow peril", and its novelty lies in combining them.[9]

With regard to the first of these discourses, scholar of religions Reza Aslan criticizes "this ill-conceived theory" for "transforming the countless cultures of the Arab and Muslim world – from Morocco to Malaysia – into a single, homo-

---

7 Huntington 1997: 29.

8 Nussbaum 2007: 6-7.

9 Nederveen Pieterse 2009: 45-46.

geneous, and historically inevitable enemy". But Aslan also lets us glimpse the controversy from another angle. Referring to his conversations with Egyptian students at the American University in Cairo in the summer after 9/11, he mentions that the talk there was all about Huntington's book, "which, though published several years before, had become a surprise bestseller in Cairo". The students, he says, "loved the book", mainly because "it seemed to them that Huntington had placed 'Islamic civilization' on a par with 'Western civilization' in his imagined global clash".[10]

Civilizations and Conflict

Like the students in Cairo, many people outside of the West have found Huntington's ideas empowering. Clash or no clash, Huntington saw non-Western civilizations as forces to be reckoned with. According to the former Singaporean diplomat Kishore Mahbubani, Huntington "effectively described" a world order where the "reluctance of leading Western minds to acknowledge the unsustainability of Western global domination presents a great danger".[11]

Not all Asians share Mahbubani's appreciation of Huntington. The Indian economist and philosopher Amartya Sen opposes all "civilizational partitioning" as reductionist. In *Identity and Violence* he underlines the dangers of rigid and unique categorizations of people, even when accompanied by well-intended appeals for dialogue. Critiquing Huntington, he argues against any form of singular classification and calls for the cultivation of plural affiliations. But Huntington himself speaks of "multiple identities which may compete with or reinforce each other", though his emphasis is on the mutual reinforcement of different levels of identity.[12] Sen, in contrast,

10 Aslan 2009: 157-59.

11 Mahbubani 2008: 7.

12 Huntington 1997: 43, 128.

nature of much of this conflict. On the other hand, he himself admits that

> the sources of conflict between states and groups from different civilizations are, in large measure, those which have always generated conflict between groups: control of people, territory, wealth and resources, and relative power, that is the ability to impose one's own values, culture, and institutions on another group as compared to that group's ability to do that to you.

But he adds, returning to his main thesis:

> Conflict between cultural groups, however, may also involve cultural issues. . . . Differences in material interest can be negotiated and often settled by compromise in a way cultural issues cannot.[17]

There is considerable truth in this. Yet it is far from certain that the degree of cultural distance between groups, by itself, has much effect on the probability or intensity of conflict. In this light the "clash of civilizations" scenario becomes questionable, even if civilizations are acknowledged and the heightened role of cultural differences in the contemporary world is accepted.

Minor Differences and Ethnic Hatred

Huntington does not take into account the "narcissism of minor differences". Fierce, even genocidal clashes can occur between very similar groups – as in Rwanda, for instance. Comparatively superficial differences appear to be all that is required for full-blown ethnic hatred; the more radical differences that exist between civilizations are hardly needed. As the Canadian politician and historian Michael Ignatieff comments,

> the level of hostility and intolerance between groups bears no relation to the size of their cultural, historical, or physical

[17] Huntington 1997: 129-30.

> differences, as measured by a dispassionate outside observer.[18]

Sigmund Freud introduced the concept of the narcissism of minor differences in a psychoanalytical context in 1917. A few years later he extended it to group psychology, remarking:

> Closely related races keep one another at arm's length; the South German cannot endure the North German, the Englishman casts every kind of aspersion upon the Scot, the Spaniard despises the Portuguese.[19]

Freud subsequently returned to this phenomenon and explained it in terms of the group-cohesion produced by directing aggression outside of the community.

The Indian philosopher Sri Aurobindo had made a similar observation in a different context:

> We know . . . that nations closely connected by every apparent tie, are actually divided by stronger antipathies than those . . . which separate them from peoples who have with them no tie of affinity.

He illustrated this with the examples of Japan and China, Norway and Sweden, and the Arabs, Turks and Persians. Unlike Freud, however, Sri Aurobindo was struck by the artificiality of this "strong, if irrational sentiment" and the ease with which it might be dissolved by eliminating the real "causes of hostility", including political and economic factors. "But these antipathies really persist," he pointed out, "only so long as there is some actual unfriendly pressure or sense of subjugation or domination or fear of the oppression of the individuality of one by the other; once that is removed they would be likely to disappear."[20]

---

18 Ignatieff 1998: 50.

19 Freud 1959: 42.

20 Aurobindo 1998b: 164. The chapter in which these sentences occur was first published in February 1917.

Skepticism about the inevitability of such animosities is supported by recent research summarized in a survey of the literature on the narcissism of minor differences (NMD) in relation to ethnic conflict. After quoting an example from the Turkish political scientist Türkkaya Ataöv, Pål Kolstø points out:

> it is clear that the hostility did not *stem* from the minor differences, instead, the conflicts are caused by something else. Members of different groups seize upon the minor differences in order to expand the identity gap between them and justify their mutual hostility.

In concluding his discussion of NMD, Kolstø notes that

> many of the authors who try to make use of it . . . end up by pointing to factors other than NMD as just as important or even more important when they explain particular conflicts. Among such other factors we have encountered status anxiety, power relations, the political context, and economic competition.[21]

Culture is often made a scapegoat for quarrels that have other roots. Much so-called ethnic violence can be understood, for instance, by taking into account the phenomenon of "market-dominant minorities". As legal scholar Amy Chua has shown, this makes the indiscriminate, simultaneous promotion of free markets and democracy around the world a dangerous policy. In many countries it can lead to the situation where a successful ethnic minority finds itself at the mercy of an impoverished, resentful and vengeful majority running the government. Chua describes the bloodbath resulting from the democratization of Rwanda in the early 1990s as one example among many. She also points out that even the virulence of global anti-Americanism, which many Americans were shocked to become aware of for the first time in September

---

21 Kolstø 2007: 161, 166-67. Italics in original.

2001, is analogous to the hatred of disproportionately prosperous minorities in individual countries.[22]

Many current conflicts can be explained more convincingly by this kind of analysis than by blaming cultural differences which may distract attention from the real causes. Culture is only part of a complex problem. But if civilizations, the largest generally recognized cultural units, do not help us as much as Huntington thought in interpreting and predicting post-Cold War conflicts, it does not follow that it is meaningless or irrelevant to speak of them. Perhaps Huntington draws our attention to the right thing for the wrong reasons. Civilizations, after all, are repositories of humanity's highest achievements through the ages. They enshrine the beauty and wisdom of its arts, philosophies, ethics and spirituality. Their diversity multiplies the resources available to us for meeting the challenges of the present. Their cooperation, not their conflict, their clasp rather than their clash may hold the key to the future.

---

[22] Chua 2004.

4

Pluralism and the Clasp of Civilizations

If thy Lord had willed, He would have made humankind into a single nation, but they will not cease to be diverse.

– Qur'an 11.118 in Abou El Fadl 2005: 207

I know that this world must go on working, wheel within wheel, this intricate mass of machinery, most complex, most wonderful. What can we do then? We can make it run smoothly, we can lessen the friction, we can grease the wheels, as it were. How? By recognising the natural necessity of variation. Just as we have recognised unity by our very nature, so we must also recognise variation. We must learn that truth may be expressed in a hundred thousand ways, and that each of these ways is true as far as it goes.

– Swami Vivekananda 1989, vol. 2: 382-83

The Paradox of Religion

THROUGHOUT history, religion has brought out the best and the worst in humanity. It has encouraged idealism and self-sacrifice and lent itself to obscurantism and intolerance. It has sanctioned wisdom and dogmatism, compassion and cruelty. Nothing has been more divisive than religion, yet it has given us our most inspiring visions of human unity. Many would be happy if this seeming relic of premodern irrationalism were to disappear from the face of the earth. But despite all expectations of its decline, religion shows few signs of dying out with the advance of modernity. In fact, it has been enjoying an almost worldwide resurgence.

If we are going to have to live with it, perhaps we should ask how this apparently inextinguishable human propensity can be turned to good use. "Religions, like all strong convictions, are a powerful force," observes the Islamic jurist Khaled Abou El Fadl, "they have the ability to thrust people toward an abyss of hate or carry them to unprecedented heights of love and enlightenment." Each religion has this contradictory potential. No feature of the religion itself determines which of the opposite tendencies will prevail; "it is left to those who describe themselves as the followers of that religion," Abou El Fadl points out, "to exploit the potential in any particular way."[1]

Much of the problem lies in attitudes toward religious differences. When our own beliefs and practices are thought to have a unique divine sanction, departures from them may seem not merely incorrect or misguided, but sinful and evil. Demonization of the other follows logically from religious exclusivism. We naturally think that God is on our side when what we call God is our own idea of Him. As the thirteenth-century Andalusian philosopher and mystic Ibn al-'Arabi put it:

> Every believer has a Lord in his heart that he has brought into existence, so he believes in Him. . . . They worship nothing but what they themselves have carved. That is why, when God discloses Himself in other than that mark, they are confounded.[2]

Conflicts involving religion are among the most intractable. Sometimes they last for centuries. "To conflict analysts," remarks Richard Rubenstein, a specialist in conflict resolution, "intense religious conflict is still a great mystery. Virtually none of us predicted the current upsurge in violent doctrinal

[1] Abou El Fadl 2005: 275.

[2] Ibn al-'Arabi, *Futûhât al-Makkiyya* IV.391.12, tr. in Chittick 1994: 151.

that religious divisions, like other differences, would fade away as the result of an increasing and eventually unanimous adoption of the creed at the heart of Western culture.

Events in the last century or so have moved in another direction, however. Neither the Christian nor the secular version of Western civilization now looks likely to extinguish the irrepressible diversity of the human race. Today this diversity, the product of thousands of years of cultural evolution, is reaffirming itself under new conditions. Historically, one of the first indications of its resurgence could be seen in Chicago as far back as 1893.

On 21 September of that year, the *St. Louis Observer* reported with alarm the impression made by Anagarika Dharmapala, the young Buddhist monk from what was then Ceylon:

> With his black, curly locks thrown back from his broad brow, his keen, clear eye fixed upon the audience, his long brown fingers emphasizing the utterances of his vibrant voice, . . . one trembled to know that such a figure stood at the head of the movement to consolidate all the disciples of Buddha and to spread "the light of Asia" throughout the civilized world.[23]

Another newspaper reported about Dharmapala:

> The Buddhist representative has created quite a furor in Chicago, . . . has a hypnotic influence over crowds and astounds his listeners with his frank criticism.[24]

Judging from this and other accounts of the effect that the Asian delegates to the Parliament had on the American public, it appears that the days of the "overpowering, unidirectional impact of the West" on every other culture were nearing an end. Some trembled. Others were delighted.

---

23 Sangharakshita 1983: 62.

24 Editorial in *Hinduism Today*, 1 November 1993, accessed on 21 April 2014, http://www.hinduismtoday.com/modules/smartsection/makepdf.php?itemid=1070.

The Delight of Difference

The sensation created by some of the Buddhist speakers at the Parliament was a sign of things to come. A notable figure besides Dharmapala was Soyen Shaku, representing Zen Buddhism. After returning to Japan he sent a student of his, D.T. Suzuki, to America. Suzuki arrived in the United States in 1897. Emulating St. Paul, he made himself Zen Buddhism's "apostle to the gentiles". He came to know many of the leading intellectuals and artists of the day, including such diverse personalities as the psychologist Erich Fromm, the Christian mystic Thomas Merton and the composer John Cage. His acknowledged impact on them exemplifies some of the varied effects of Eastern culture on the American mind in the twentieth century. Zen became a household word. Adapted by Suzuki to Western needs, as George Leonard observes, "it swept with equal ease through the artworld, the universities, the educated public".[25]

Once Asians had recovered from the initial shock of the European assault on their cultures, the propagation of Christianity by Western missionaries provided a model for some of the more enterprising among them. The Parliament of Religions launched a number of movements spreading Eastern philosophical and spiritual teachings to America and Europe. No longer were the peoples of the East just recipients of the impact of the West.

The competition for converts made for a better intercultural balance than the previous one-way flow of influence from an aggressive West to a passive East. The missionary spirit itself, however, is not typically Asian. Proselytism reflects attitudes toward religious differences that have been less prevalent in the East than in the West. It is driven by an assumption of the superior value of what is being promoted, whether what it tries to replace is seen as false and evil or merely as incomplete

---

[25] Leonard 1994: 151.

> assembly as "Sisters and Brothers of America", a deafening applause of two minutes followed, and then I proceeded; and when it was finished, I sat down almost exhausted with emotion.[29]

Vivekananda spoke of belonging to a religion that acknowledges all paths to God. Thanking the audience "in the name of millions and millions of Hindu people", he declared:

> We believe not only in universal toleration, but we accept all religions as true.

He ended his impromptu remarks with an impassioned appeal for peace, harmony and mutual understanding:

> Sectarianism, bigotry, and its horrible descendant, fanaticism, have long possessed this beautiful earth. They have filled the earth with violence. . . . I fervently hope that the bell that tolled this morning in honour of this convention may be the death-knell of all fanaticism, of all persecutions with the sword or with the pen, and of all uncharitable feelings between persons wending their way to the same goal.[30]

When the young man from India began to speak, one woman afterwards recalled, thousands "rose to their feet as a tribute to something they knew not what".[31] Vivekananda spoke from the heart and people responded from the heart. A surge of feeling swept through the crowd. We may call it the delight of difference.

Images, Crosses and Crescents

Considering how closely Vivekananda's name is linked to the Parliament of Religions, it is ironic that he was turned away when he first presented himself as a prospective speaker. He

---

29 Vivekananda 1989, vol. 5: 20-21.

30 Barrows 1893, vol. 1: 102.

31 Burke 1992, vol. 1: 81.

had sailed from India at the end of May 1893, and arrived in Chicago late in July. Inquiring at the information bureau of the World's Columbian Exposition, he learned that the Parliament had been postponed to September. But he was not sponsored by an organization and had no formal credentials; in any case, he was told, it was too late for him to be registered as a delegate. No one had thought of such details when his admirers in India arranged for him to travel to America to represent their religion at this international event. Vivekananda ended up going to Boston, where J.H. Wright, a professor of Greek at Harvard, was impressed by his intellect and wrote to friends in Chicago. In this roundabout way he came finally to be accepted as a representative of Hinduism.[32]

The charismatic thirty-year-old swami, born Narendranath Datta, had received a Western-style education in Calcutta, then the capital of British India. Under the influence of the great Bengali saint Sri Ramakrishna, he had discarded his early religious skepticism and plunged into the spiritual life. After Ramakrishna's passing, he walked the length and breadth of India for several years as a wandering ascetic, mixing with the common people as the country groaned under the weight of colonial rule. In Chicago he first presented to the world at large the synthesis that took shape in his mind in response to these varied experiences. His interpretation of Hinduism was to have an incalculable impact on modern understandings of it.

Swami Vivekananda's most substantial contribution to the Parliament was his "Paper on Hinduism", delivered on 19 September. He spoke neither as a traditionalist nor as a scholar, but as a practitioner of an ancient religion coming to grips with modernity. He placed his own religion in the context of the relationship of all religions to the ultimate reality that justifies their existence:

---

32 Nikhilananda 1964: 125-28.

> To the Hindu, man is not travelling from error to truth, but from truth to truth, from lower to higher truth. To him all the religions . . . mean so many attempts of the human soul to grasp and realise the Infinite. . . . Unity in variety is the plan of nature, and the Hindu has recognised it. . . . The Hindus have discovered that the absolute can only be realised, or thought of, or stated, through the relative, and the images, crosses, and crescents are simply so many symbols. . . . Every religion is only evolving a God out of the material man, and the same God is the inspirer of all of them.[33]

Evolution was a central theme of the Columbian Exposition as a whole, as inclusivism was of the Parliament of Religions. But just as this inclusivism meant welcoming non-Christians as potential converts to Christianity, so evolution was understood to be a process that had culminated in the rationalistic enlightenment and material development of the modern West, to which less advanced peoples were invited to aspire. Vivekananda engaged with these two ideas in a manner that turned the intention behind the Exposition and the Parliament on its head.

In the architecture of the Exposition, the climax of evolutionary progress was symbolized by the White City, soon to be immortalized in the "alabaster cities" of the song "America the Beautiful". The Midway Plaisance, in contrast, was the site of a sort of ethnological zoo where living specimens of humanity's racial and cultural diversity were on exhibit. Its purpose, in the words of an editorial in the *Los Angeles Times* on 20 September 1893, was to remind visitors "that millions are yet between savagery and civilization, and that a stupendous work has yet to be accomplished before the race, as a whole, shall be fit for self-government and permanent civili-zation".[34] The juxtaposition of the White City and the Midway Plaisance

---

33 Vivekananda 1989, vol. 1: 17-18.

34 Seager 1995: 24.

conveyed a vision of America's place in the scheme of things that drew millions to one of the most ambitious fairs in history. As Richard Seager explains in his book on the Parliament of Religions, situating the East–West encounter that occurred there in the context of the Columbian Exposition:

> The White City signified the highly evolved, the progressive, the modern, the enlightened, the West, or the truly universal, while the Midway stood for those who were the less evolved, the backward or out-of-date, the unenlightened or superstitious, the East, or the merely particular.[35]

Seager adds that the "inclusion and subordination" of these other people "played a critical role in creating the mystique of the White City":

> Without them, the Exposition would have been little more than an in-group celebration by the imperial nations of the West at a trade fair hosted by a young comer eager to break into the front rank. With them, the Exposition became an image of the world that suggested to many Americans how truly liberal, progressive, and enlightened they had become.[36]

Though Vivekananda admired many things about America as he experienced it in the last decade of the nineteenth century, he had a different image of the world in his mind than the one evoked by the Columbian Exposition. He did not reject evolution and progress, however; rather, he enlarged and transformed their significance. "No rational man can possibly quarrel with these evolutionists," he said in a lecture after the Parliament, but we "have to go one step further."[37] This further step redefined progress and evolution in spiritual terms. Thus an "Eastern" turn was given to ideas at the heart of the Western ideology of modernism.

---

35 Seager 1995: 25.

36 Ibid.: 39.

37 Vivekananda 1989, vol. 2: 207.

"Every religion is only evolving a God out of the material man", Vivekananda declared in his "Paper on Hinduism". This assertion challenged both the Eurocentric evolutionism of the Exposition and the Christian inclusivism behind the Parliament. If human evolution is the unfolding of the divinity within us, the achievements displayed in the White City could represent no more than a midway point in this process. Perhaps they even showed a relapse toward the "material man". Upsetting the hierarchical ranking of the White City and the Midway, Vivekananda demolished at one stroke nineteenth-century Western man's claim to stand on the top rung of the evolutionary ladder.

"And the same God is the inspirer of all of them", he continued. As the religious historian Leigh Schmidt observes, Vivekananda "managed to turn the tables on the era's more conventional Protestants who thought the whole 'heathen' gathering should be imbued with a Christian missionary logic".[38] This much is uncontroversial. Most of the missionaries themselves considered the Parliament a disaster. Though a number of Asians shared the responsibility for this outcome, Vivekananda was perhaps more to blame than anyone else. There is disagreement, however, about whether he himself advocated what we would now call pluralism, a reverse inclusivism or some combination of them. His own words have been quoted in support of conflicting interpretations of his outlook. One view is that he was not really a pluralist at all, but a Vedantic inclusivist and a "missionary" of his brand of Hinduism. His reputation as a ground-breaking pluralist has sometimes been undermined by his supporters as much as by his detractors.

It is true that Vivekananda's powerful personality occasionally reacted to aggression against his religion and

38 Schmidt 2005: 162-63.

culture with an assertion not only of equality, but of superiority. It must be remembered that the useful, though not entirely unproblematic, distinction between religious exclusivism, inclusivism and pluralism would not be made explicit for decades to come. Perfect consistency in maintaining an orientation that did not yet have a name could hardly be expected. But at least as regards Vivekananda's role in the Parliament and in the broad changes it initiated or encouraged, the most memorable feature of his approach to religious differences was his articulation of a pluralism that was well ahead of its time in the global religious scene.

In his "Paper on Hinduism", we may recall, Vivekananda spoke of religions as "so many attempts of the human soul to grasp and realise the Infinite". He credited the Hindus with having "discovered that the absolute can only be realised, or thought of, or stated, through the relative", so that "the images, crosses, and crescents are simply so many symbols". It would be hard to find a clearer statement of religious pluralism in the nineteenth century. Vivekananda's pluralism was inspired by the long Indian tradition of acceptance of religious diversity and more specifically by the example and teaching of his *guru*, Sri Ramakrishna. Receiving intensive media exposure as a result of the Parliament in Chicago, Vivekananda's words created a stir at the time and pointed toward the emergence of a more pluralistic religious liberalism in the century that followed.

Religious Differences and World Peace

If modernity had secularized the world by now or at least confined religion to private life, as was once expected, religious differences would matter little today except among the dwindling number who still clung to traditional beliefs and practices. But by the 1970s, the secularization theories of social scientists began to be massively falsified by events. The religious resurgence has been described by a number of commentators, such as the French political scientist Gilles Kepel in a provocatively titled book, *The Revenge of God* (*La Revanche de Dieu*). Kepel writes:

> It is the logic of conflict which underlies the parallel development of different religious movements setting out to reconquer the world. Such conflict is ultimately a war between 'believers' who make the reaffirmation of their religious identity into the criterion of truths that are both exclusive of others and peculiar to themselves.[39]

Exclusivism is not the only religious option, however, and religions need not obey the logic of conflict in their relationships with each other or with the secular world. *The Revenge of God* seems to accept the claims of fundamentalists to represent their religions and speak on behalf of God. In the case of Islam, whose reputation has suffered the most from such claims, another viewpoint is offered by Khaled Abou El Fadl in *The Great Theft: Wrestling Islam from the Extremists*. "While puritans wage violent jihad", Abou El Fadl exhorts his co-religionists, "to win this war, moderates must engage in the superior form of jihad – a peaceful jihad. Unless moderate Muslims realize that they are in a state of intellectual jihad over the future of Islam, they will never match the unrelenting zeal of the puritans."[40] Much the same situation exists in other religions with militant minorities.

On 11 September 1893, inaugurating the world's first Parliament of Religions, Charles Bonney declared:

> when the religious faiths of the world recognize each other as brothers, . . . then, and not till then, will the nations of the earth yield to the spirit of concord and learn war no more.[41]

Considering how little the colossal bloodbaths of the twentieth century had to do with religion, this was clearly an insufficient

39 Kepel 1994: 203.

40 Abou El Fadl 2005: 286.

41 Barrows 1893, vol. 1: 67; Seager and Kidd 1993: 17.

prescription for abolishing war. But in recent years and especially in the aftermath of a more recent September 11, the call for a brotherhood of faiths – now known as religious pluralism – has acquired a new urgency.

The intransigence of self-proclaimed defenders of God is a major factor in the intractability of many post-Cold War conflicts. Even apart from violent fanaticism, all exclusivism is inherently divisive; nor is religious inclusivism as unifying as it pretends to be. As the Indian Christian theologian Stanley Samartha put it:

> Exclusiveness regards universality as the extension of its own particularity and seeks to conquer other faiths. Inclusiveness, though seeming generous, actually co-opts other faiths without their leave. Both exclusiveness and its patronizing cousin inclusiveness may even be forms of theological violence against neighbors of other faiths and, when combined with economic, political, and military power, as has often happened in history, become dangerous to communal harmony and world peace.[42]

If religion is to survive and play a constructive role in the global age, it can only be on the basis of a pluralistic ethos. In a post-9/11 talk in Tehran, John Hick, a British theologian and noted proponent of religious pluralism, reformulated the gist of Bonney's appeal at the Parliament of 1893:

> Today, to insist on the unique superiority of your own faith is to be part of the problem. . . . The only stable and enduring basis for peace will come about when dialogue leads to a mutual acceptance of the world religions as different but equally valid relationships to the ultimate reality.[43]

---

[42] Samartha 1987: 79.

[43] John Hick, "Religious Pluralism and Islam" (lecture at the Institute for Islamic Culture and Thought, Tehran, February 2005), accessed on 21 April 2014, http://www.johnhick.org.uk/article11.html. Hick quotes not Bonney's words, but a more recent statement to the same effect by the ecumenical theologian Hans Küng.

Religion, Culture and Globalization

Religion is part of culture, though religions with universalistic tendencies may break away from their roots in particular cultures. Culture itself is sometimes defined to entail exclusion, making the notion of intercultural understanding and cooperation problematic. The religious historian Bruce Lincoln describes culture as "the prime instrument through which groups mobilize themselves, construct their collective identity, and effect their solidarity by excluding those whom they identify as outsiders". Religion can energize these exclusionary functions of culture and invest them with unquestionable authority. Lincoln goes on to offer an explanation of the centrality of religion to most traditional cultures:

> In the form of routinized practices mandated and supported by religious discourse, a community's characteristic preferences are experienced as sacred duties, not simply human choices. For better and also for worse, the more thoroughly a community's preferences can be encompassed within the religious, the more stable that community becomes.

The worse side of this stability can become evident in a rapidly changing world when diverse religions and cultures are thrown together to adapt to each other as best they can. Lincoln points out with reference to the present religious resurgence:

> Restoring religion to its dominant position within culture . . . simply ensures that a culture's most bruising conflicts will assume religious . . . character, and in that form they can be more destructive than ever. When one rejects the Enlightenment's values en masse and dispenses with its model of culture, one risks not just a return of the repressed, but novel Wars of Religion.[44]

---

[44] Lincoln 2003: 52, 56, 61.

But the idea that cultural clashes can be avoided only by propagating Enlightenment values assumes that culture – apart from modern Western culture – is inherently exclusive. Some scholars object to defining culture in terms of exclusion and difference. By starting with such a definition, the sociologist Jan Nederveen Pieterse argues, we have already "defined any form of intergroup or transnational culture out of existence". Emphasizing hybridization and the "global mélange", he prefers a concept of culture as

> behavior and beliefs that are learned and shared: learned so it is not 'instinctual' and shared so it is not individual. Sharing refers to social sharing but there is no limitation as to the boundaries of this sociality. No territorial or historical boundaries are implied as part of the definition.[45]

This view of culture readily accommodates hybridity and convergence. However, it leaves the future of diversity open to question.

Since the age of colonialism, the world has been partially homogenized by the cultural inclusivism of Western modernity. "Civilization is making the whole world one", the good bishop said in the late nineteenth century. By civilization he meant, of course, modern Western civilization. At one time this was expected to spread Christianity wherever it went. But the advent of secularism relegated religion to a secondary role in the diffusion of Western culture. The recent global religious upsurge has been associated more with de-Westernization, despite a high rate of conversions to evangelical Protestantism in some parts of Asia, Africa and Latin America. The world continues to become one and is now being de-secularized, but on the whole it is becoming neither Western nor Christian. Cultures and religions show few signs of shedding some of their deepest differences as

45 Nederveen Pieterse 2009: 47-48.

their interaction intensifies. Under such circumstances, collective harmony will depend on a willingness to accept these differences, even to celebrate them.

Attitudes toward religious differences tend to reflect and reinforce attitudes toward cultural differences in general. Thus religious exclusivism often goes hand in hand with what we may term cultural exclusivism. Likewise religious inclusivism and pluralism frequently accompany cultural inclusivism and pluralism, respectively. In some contexts, these various cultural attitudes or policies are called nativism, assimilationism and multiculturalism.

Since religious and cultural differences commonly coincide, attitudes toward both are sometimes studied together using these or equivalent categories. "The terms *exclusion*, *assimilation*, and *pluralism* suggest three different ways in which Americans have approached our ever broader cultural and religious diversity",[46] writes the comparative religionist Diana Eck in an account of the increasingly multireligious and multicultural society of the United States. Roughly the same options are available for dealing with the global diversity now pressing more and more on our consciousness.

Cultural or religious exclusivism in modern times is a rejectionist response to unprecedented exposure to mental outlooks and ways of life different from our own. It can also be a self-defensive reaction to cultural globalization as a homogenizing force whose inclusivism tolerates differences only to undermine them. People and cultures are now being mixed together in a sort of worldwide melting pot. But Eck points out an ambiguity in this metaphor for assimilation as it was once popularly envisaged in America:

> Is it basically an Anglo-conformist melting pot in which the races of the rest of Europe are assimilated? Is it more a

---

46 Eck 2002: 47. Italics in original.

> transmuting pot in which everybody changes in the mix? The melting pot image is used in both ways.[47]

The same questions can be asked about the inclusivism of cultural globalization.

Globalization as Westernization or Americanization (analogous to the Anglo-conformist interpretation of the early-twentieth-century American melting pot) is much less acceptable to non-Westerners and non-Americans than a more symmetrical and egalitarian convergence would be. But in any case, the melting pot model has been abandoned even in the United States itself and there is far less prospect of thoroughly homogenizing humankind. All indications are that cultural and religious diversity will be with us for the foreseeable future. Pluralism embraces this reality and tries to turn it to the advantage of all.

The Crisis of the World-System

Globalization has made it possible today, as never before, to conceive of the entire human race as a single community. But economic globalization in its current form is as divisive as it is unifying. The West's dominance over much of the rest of humanity in the colonial era has mutated into inequalities between North and South as well as between globalization's winners and losers within every society. These disparities have given rise to what political scientist Manfred Steger describes as an "ideological contest over the meaning and shape of globalization" which "has deeply impacted the political landscape of the new century".[48]

Steger distinguishes "*globalization* – a set of social processes of increasing interdependence" from "*globalisms* – political ideologies . . . that endow globalization with their preferred

---

[47] Eck 2002: 56.

[48] Steger 2009: 5.

norms, values, and meanings".[49] The ideology he refers to as market globalism now dominates the discourse and determines what globalization means to most people, whether or not they accept its whole agenda. It tries to persuade us that globalization is an inevitable process of economic liberalization and integration whose long-term results – whatever the immediate appearances – will be beneficial to all. Two main alternative ideologies dispute this claim. Steger calls them justice globalism and jihadist globalism. Armed with very different perceptions of what globalization is about and where it ought to lead, the ideologies of globalism are engaged in bitter combat to decide the shape of things to come.

These contenders for the right to interpret the significance of globalization and direct its course exhibit the three approaches to human diversity we have encountered. The prevailing neoliberal view of globalization, identifying it with free-market economics, is inherently inclusive. "There is no activity more intrinsically globalizing than trade, no ideology less interested in nations than capitalism, no challenge to frontiers more audacious than the market", observes Benjamin Barber in *Jihad vs. McWorld*. "A consumer is a consumer is a consumer",[50] he adds, stressing the inclusive nature of an economic ideology that defines us all, whether we like it or not, as consumers. The cultural concomitant of this ideology, often characterized as the Americanization of the world, is equally inclusive. It has brought about to a limited extent and in relatively superficial ways the homogenization of humanity which some hope and others fear will be the result of cultural globalization. But like religious inclusivism, this cultural inclusivism hides many lurking exclusions and is unacceptable to those who do not want to be assimilated.

---

49 Steger 2009: 17. Italics in original.

50 Barber 1996: 23.

Market globalism enjoyed a moment of apparent triumph in the 1990s after the breakdown of Soviet Communism. Meanwhile it had provoked widespread fundamentalist reactions, including the violence of Global Jihad. The collapse of the Twin Towers of the World Trade Center on September 11, 2001, brought home to many people the worldwide reach of this Islamic form of counter-globalism. Jihadism, as Reza Aslan points out, for all its claims to doctrinal purity, derives not from the Qur'an but from the writings of the thirteenth-century cleric Ibn Taymiyyah. The world-view of this globalist ideology is sharply exclusive. Jihadists, Aslan says,

> put forth a simple proposition: The universe is divided into two. . . . There is no middle ground. If you are not on one side, then you are on the other. If you are not *us*, then you are *them*. . . . In a cosmic war one is either with God or against God.[51]

But Jihadism is only one manifestation of the hostility provoked by neoliberal globalization and perceived neocolonialism. By promising more than it can deliver, market globalism may continue to generate new forms of militant rejectionism. In a worst-case scenario, the bleak picture painted by the Indian writer Pankaj Mishra could prove prophetic:

> The hope that fuels the pursuit of endless economic growth – that billions of consumers in India and China will one day enjoy the lifestyles of Europeans and Americans – is as absurd and dangerous a fantasy as anything dreamt up by al-Qaeda. It condemns the global environment to early destruction, and looks set to create reservoirs of nihilistic rage and disappointment among hundreds of millions of have-nots.[52]

---

51 Aslan 2009: xviii, 102-03. Italics in original.

52 Mishra 2012: 309-10.

The hegemonic globalism of the market is challenged from another side by the global justice movement, whose "affirmation of a 'global we'", Steger observes, is "tied to its irreducible plurality and diversity".[53] "We are building a world where diversity is considered an asset and individuality a source of richness", asserts the Women's Global Charter for Humanity. Quoting this and other statements of the pluralism of the alter-globalization movement, Geoffrey Pleyers comments:

> This valorization of diversity . . . constitutes a recurring argument evoked by alter-globalization activists to distinguish themselves from, and to oppose, communalism, fundamentalism or nationalism as well as neoliberalism.[54]

Proposing an alternative to neoliberal globalization, the World Social Forum has timed most of its annual gatherings, since its inauguration in 2001 in Porto Alegre, Brazil, to coincide with the meetings of corporate and political leaders at the World Economic Forum in Davos, Switzerland. "Another world is possible", proclaims the WSF. The sociologist and political economist Immanuel Wallerstein finds in this slogan a significant expression of the "sense that the world-system is in a structural crisis, and that political options are real". Alluding to the venues associated with the two forums, he adds:

> The world is facing increasingly a struggle on many fronts between the spirit of Davos and the spirit of Porto Alegre.

He goes on to mention a third party to the contest:

> The dramatic attack by Osama bin Laden on the Twin Towers on September 11, 2001, marked a further indication of world political chaos.[55]

---

53 Steger 2009: 127.

54 Pleyers 2010: 27.

55 Wallerstein 2004: 86-87.

Thus the three competing ideologies of globalism discussed by Steger, with their contrasting attitudes toward diversity, also figure in Wallerstein's analysis of the crisis of the world-system.

What does such a crisis portend for the system? Wallerstein explains in the terminology of systems theory:

> To use the technical language of natural science, what happens is that the system bifurcates. . . . We can translate this into everyday language by saying that the system is faced with two alternative solutions for its crisis, both of which are intrinsically possible. In effect, the members of the system collectively are called upon to make a historical choice about which of the alternative paths will be followed, that is, what kind of new system will be constructed.[56]

World-systems analysis draws on similarities between social systems and natural systems in an attempt to understand the behavior of the largest of all social systems. The Belgian–Russian chemist and Nobel laureate Ilya Prigogine and his colleague Isabelle Stengers, describing bifurcating systems on the basis of work on chemical dissipative structures, endorse this cross-disciplinary parallelism from the scientific side:

> Such systems seem to "hesitate" among various possible directions of evolution. . . . A small fluctuation may start an entirely new evolution that will drastically change the whole behavior of the macroscopic system. The analogy with social phenomena, even with history, is inescapable.[57]

In the present world crisis, what are the possible directions we have to choose between? The ideologies of globalization seem to offer three alternatives. However, Wallerstein treats global jihad not as offering an alternative solution, but as an instance of the wild oscillations predicted by systems theory in the chaotic process of bifurcation. This would leave us to

56 Wallerstein 2004: 76.

57 Prigogine and Stengers 1985: 14.

decide between two main options. Globalization as it is stands accused of increasing the clout of transnational corporations, aggravating inequalities, undermining democracy, generating instability, endangering our environment and homogenizing culture. On the other side is a growing, heterogeneous movement with the mantra, "Another world is possible".

Toward a One-World Dynamic

Humankind, declared Sri Aurobindo, "is undergoing an evolutionary crisis in which is concealed a choice of its destiny".[58] We live, he said, in "the hour of the unexpected, the incalculable, the immeasurable". It is one of those "periods when even a little effort produces great results and changes destiny", in contrast to "spaces of time when much labour goes to the making of a little result".[59]

Systems theorists in the West have made observations strikingly similar in substance to those of the Indian seer. Contrasting critical moments in the life of a system with normal times, Wallerstein notes that

> two things are true at these points of bifurcation: small inputs have large outputs (as opposed to times of the normal development of a system when large inputs have small outputs); and the outcome of such bifurcations is inherently indeterminate.

In these "periods of transition from one historical system to another one", as Wallerstein sees it, "human struggle takes on the most meaning". Putting it differently,

> it is only in such times of transition that what we call free will outweighs the pressures of the existing system to return to equilibria. Thus, fundamental change is possible albeit never certain, and this fact makes claims on our moral

58 Aurobindo 2005a: 1090.

59 Aurobindo 1997a: 146.

> responsibility to act rationally, in good faith, and with strength to seek a better historical system.[60]

We are at a fork in the road of history. The prophets of doom are legion and they have good reasons for their pessimism. The world-system might break down altogether. Or it may break through out of the present world-disorder to a new order. Since our individual choices could make a difference, we have to think about what kind of global society we want. If another world is possible, what kind of world do we want it to be and what are the conditions for creating it?

Economic and political issues loom large among the problems to be solved. But economics and politics operate in cultural contexts which can no longer be ignored. Let us recall Huntington's pithy formula:

> In a multicivilizational world, the constructive course is to renounce universalism, accept diversity, and seek commonalities.

Honoring cultural differences, the search for commonalities is to replace the imposition of universalism as a glue to hold things together. Huntington explains:

> Instead of promoting the supposedly universal features of one civilization, the requisites for cultural coexistence demand a search for what is common to most civilizations.

He draws on Michael Walzer's distinction between "thick" and "thin" or maximalist and minimalist morality to suggest the nature of some of the commonalities we can expect to find, including concepts of truth and justice and injunctions against murder, deceit and tyranny. The exploration of such commonalities, Huntington believes, will go some distance

60 Immanuel Wallerstein, "Uncertainty and Creativity" (talk at *Forum 2000: Concerns and Hopes on the Threshold of the New Millennium*, Prague, 3-6 September 1997), accessed on 21 April 2014, http://www2.binghamton.edu/fbc/archive/iwuncer.htm.

The Clasp of Civilizations?

Distinct cultures will undoubtedly continue to flourish despite globalization. At the same time, the sense of human unity may grow ever more compelling under the pressure of closer and closer interactions. But the same pressure could also multiply and magnify cultural conflicts. To some extent this is what has been happening so far. Huntington assumed that the differences between civilizations, being the largest, would cause the worst clashes. However, as the Ghanaian–British–American philosopher and cultural theorist Kwame Anthony Appiah points out:

> Warring parties are seldom at odds because they have clashing conceptions of "the good". On the contrary, conflict arises most often when two peoples have identified the same thing as good. . . . What makes these conflicts so intense is that they are battles over the meaning of the *same* values, not that they oppose one value, held exclusively by one side, with another, held exclusively by their antagonists.

Appiah is convinced that

> we can live in harmony without agreeing on underlying values (except, perhaps, the cosmopolitan value of living together).

He urges us to

> learn about people in other places, take an interest in their civilizations, their arguments, their errors, their achievements, not because that will bring us to agreement, but because it will help us get used to one another.[66]

Whether civilizations clash or not, Huntington made a signal contribution to political theory by stressing their contemporary relevance. For Canadian political scientist Robert Cox, "civilizations represent the ways large aggregates of people

---

66 Appiah 2007: 78, 81.

interpret the world, respond to it, and shape projects for acting in it".[67] Though he is critical of Huntington's prediction of "clashes" of civilizations, he sees in today's world a "dialectic of homogenization and diversification" in which globalization "is countered by the affirmation of civilizations".[68] Clearly some such dialectic is at work. Global integration is being vigorously countered by particularistic self-assertions. But how significant are civilizations as such in this process?

One can hardly doubt the historical importance of civilizations as sprawling cultural entities, often religiously defined, whose premodern extent in several cases exceeded that of any modern nation-state. In his classic study of the rise of nationalism, political theorist Benedict Anderson remarks:

> Few things are more impressive than the vast territorial stretch of the Ummah Islam from Morocco to the Sulu Archipelago, of Christendom from Paraguay to Japan, and of the Buddhist world from Sri Lanka to the Korean peninsula. The great sacral cultures (and for our purposes here it may be permissible to include 'Confucianism') incorporated conceptions of immense communities.[69]

Anderson also observes, however, that

> for all the grandeur and power of the great religiously imagined communities, their *unselfconscious coherence* waned steadily after the late Middle Ages.[70]

These "sacral cultures" largely corresponded to what historians call civilizations. "Almost all civilizations," according to Braudel, "are pervaded or submerged by religion, . . . and they draw from it the most powerful motives in their particular

67 Cox 2002: 11.

68 Ibid.: 1-2.

69 Anderson 1991: 12.

70 Ibid.: 16. Italics in original.

psychology." Modern Western civilization is a partial exception. Even here, however, "Christianity is an essential reality", from which many seemingly non-religious cultural features derive.[71] But the proliferation of nation-states in the last two or three centuries has coincided with the apparent decline of most of the great civilizations, though their religions survive. Is there any reason to believe that these civilizations are still forces to be reckoned with?

Huntington insists that there is. Since the end of the Cold War, he maintains, countries throughout the world "have been groping for groupings, and they are finding those groupings with countries of similar culture and the same civilization". He saw a "civilization-based world-order" emerging, in which "societies sharing cultural affinities cooperate with each other".[72] Huntington was not the first to conceive of a world-order based on groupings according to cultural affinities. Several decades earlier, Sri Aurobindo had written that "the peoples of humanity must be allowed to group themselves according to their free-will and their natural affinities". He believed that "the unity of the human race to be entirely sound and in consonance with the deepest laws of life must be founded on free groupings, and the groupings again must be the natural association of free individuals". In political terms, "the free and natural nation-unit and perhaps the nation-group would be the just and living support of a sound and harmonious world-system".[73]

Though he was writing when colonialism was at its height and such developments seemed almost unthinkable, Sri Aurobindo speculated on the future possibilities of a political arrangement that would give full weight to cultural variations.

---

[71] Braudel 1993: 23.

[72] Huntington 1997: 127, 20.

[73] Aurobindo 1998b: 270, 243, 162.

One possibility he saw included "a European grouping, an Asiatic grouping, an American grouping, with two or three sub-groups in America, Latin and English-speaking, three in Asia, the Mongolian, Indian and West-Asian, with Moslem North Africa perhaps as a natural annexe to the third of these". These groupings correspond roughly to several of Huntington's civilizations. Sri Aurobindo recognized the difficulties standing in the way of the realization of such a scheme, but thought that they "might not be of great importance under a better system of things":

> It is easily conceivable therefore that with a system in which the causes of hostility would disappear, natural affinities would prevail and a grouping of the kind imagined might become more easily practicable. It is arguable also that the trend of mankind under a great stress of tendency towards unification would naturally move to the creation of such a symmetry. It may be that a great change and revolution in the world would powerfully and rapidly abolish all the obstacles.[74]

Sri Aurobindo's ideas on the remaking of world order are surprisingly similar to Huntington's in some ways, but differ markedly in others. Less preoccupied with the risk of intercivilizational conflict, he envisioned regional groupings as a possible step toward realizing a diversified human unity. However, he admitted that under certain circumstances there could be a danger of "huge continental clashes".[75] Another difference is that he was less prone than Huntington to link civilizations with particular religions. Nor was he so disposed to treat religions as markers of mutually antagonistic identities.

The recent religious resurgence, in Huntington's view, has contributed to the revitalization of civilizations that once

---

74 Aurobindo 1998b: 163-64.

75 Ibid.: 320.

seemed almost moribund and looked easily assimilable into the supposedly universal civilization of the West. "The revival of religion," he thinks, "provides a basis for identity and commitment that transcends national boundaries and unites civilizations."[76] But if it unites civilizations, it would seem to divide humanity. Religious exclusivism in that case could be the undoing of a relentlessly globalizing world where the mutual demonizations of the past have become a dangerous anachronism. However, that is not the only role that religion and spirituality could play. The relationships between religions, like the relationships between cultures, are not intrinsically oppositional. Since the nineteenth century, religious pluralism has grown steadily alongside the contrary drift toward fundamentalism. Favored by the unavoidable interchanges of the global age, pluralism may prove to be the more enduring trend.

Ibn al-'Arabi wrote in the golden age of Islamic civilization:

> When God wants someone to attain the truth and give it its full due, He bestows upon him knowledge of His breadth and vastness and that He is witnessed in the belief of every believer.[77]

Perhaps few even today are able to give this "breadth and vastness" their full due. Yet more and more people throughout the world are willing to grant validity to beliefs other than their own. At the first Parliament of Religions, Swami Vivekananda spoke of the Hindu attitude of accepting all religions as true. Since then, mainstream religion in much of the world has moved toward a similar acceptance.

The question remains whether the unifying potential of religion can prevail over its divisive tendencies. Its power to

---

[76] Huntington 2000: 6.

[77] Ibn al-'Arabi, *Futûhât al-Makkiyya* III 309.30, tr. in Chittick 1994: 153.

sanctify irrationality points in one direction, the spiritual urge toward self-discovery and transcendence in the other. Today both are accentuated. It is yet to be seen whether the aspirations toward peace, harmony and enlightenment found in all religions will outweigh their use as tools of identity politics. But their appeal to what is best in humanity may yet trump the sectarianism, bigotry and fanaticism decried by Vivekananda on that now half-forgotten September 11, in Chicago. If so, religions as vital manifestations of human diversity could impart their ardor to a vibrant unity in difference – not a clash, but a clasp of civilizations.

5

Untold Potentialities

Jawaharlal Nehru, Sri Aurobindo and the Idea of India

Nehru saw Indian independence as part of a wider Asian resurgence. Past centuries might have belonged to Europe, or to the white races in general, but it was now time for coloured and previously subordinated peoples to come into their own.

– Ramachandra Guha 2007: 162

The modern world is still mainly European, a world dominated by the European mind and Western civilisation. We claim to set right this undue preponderance, to reassert the Asiatic and, for ourselves, the Indian mind and to preserve and develop the great values of Asiatic and of Indian civilisation.

– Sri Aurobindo 2004: 51-52

Independence and Interdependence

SHORTLY after 11 o'clock in the evening on 14 August 1947, Jawaharlal Nehru addressed the Constituent Assembly representing the nation whose first prime minister he was about to become. From the Council House in New Delhi his words were broadcast throughout the country. At the stroke of midnight, India would be free. The hour of her "tryst with destiny" had arrived. "It is a fateful moment," Nehru declared, "for us in India, for all Asia and for the world." In a cosmopolitan gesture, he asked his hearers to pledge their dedication not only "to the service of India and her people", but "to the still larger cause of humanity". He spoke of working to realize dreams that were "for India, but . . . also for the world, for all the nations and peoples are too closely knit together today for any one of them to imagine that it can live apart". The new nation, heir to an ancient civilization, was breaking away from an empire on which the sun had never set and was embarking on an independent course. Complete separateness had ceased to be a real option in this age of growing interdependence, however. Nehru observed:

> Peace has been said to be indivisible; so is freedom, so is prosperity now, and so also is disaster in this one world that can no longer be split into isolated fragments.[1]

In 1947 what we now call globalization had not yet been named, but its consequences have never been more pointedly enumerated.

Earlier on the 14th, another message was broadcast by All India Radio in Tiruchirapalli and Madras. Written by the philosopher, mystic and former nationalist leader Sri Aurobindo, who had been living since 1910 in the French colony of Pondicherry, it was equally internationalist in spirit. Sri Aurobindo had entered the freedom struggle at an early stage when, as he later recalled, most Indians regarded

> the ideal of independence . . . as unpractical and impossible, an almost insane chimera. It was thought that the British Empire was too powerful and India too weak, effectively disarmed and impotent even to dream of the success of such an endeavour.[2]

During a year in prison undergoing trial on charges of conspiracy, of which he was finally acquitted by a judge who had been his classmate at Cambridge, he had a series of inner experiences which changed the direction of his life. Some

---

1 Montefiore 2005: 120-21.

2 Aurobindo 2006: 47.

months after his release, he abruptly discontinued the political activities he had resumed and left Calcutta, going first to the nearby French enclave of Chandernagore and then to Pondicherry on the south-eastern coast of India. His withdrawal from politics was meant to be temporary at first. It became permanent, however, as his preoccupation with the possibility of transforming the human consciousness grew all-absorbing and the focus of his work for his country shifted from nationalism to expanding the horizons of India's cultural and spiritual regeneration.

Impossible Dreams

In his independence day message Sri Aurobindo, like Nehru, spoke not only of India, but of Asia and the world. August 15th as the birthday of free India signified in his vision "the entry into the comity of nations of a new power with untold potentialities which has a great part to play in determining the political, social, cultural and spiritual future of humanity". As it happened, the date fixed for India's independence coincided with his own seventy-fifth birthday. Having been asked for a message which he felt he was "perhaps hardly in a position to give", he took the occasion to make a personal statement. Certain aims and ideals he had conceived early in his life, which seemed then to be "impossible dreams", could now be observed "either approaching fruition or initiated and on the way to their achievement".[3] All of them, he believed, were relevant to India's freedom and future work. But his dreams for India were, like Nehru's, for the world as well.

India's independence was the first of these dreams. The second was closely related to it:

---

3 Aurobindo 2006: 474-75. I have quoted from the message as originally written. For the actual broadcast it had to be revised and shortened, as reproduced ibid.: 478-80.

> the resurgence and liberation of Asia and her return to the great role which she had played in the progress of human civilization.

Like a number of other Asian leaders of his generation, Sri Aurobindo was a pan-Asianist. At the same time, he was an internationalist. He expected the rise of Asia to lead not to a clash of civilizations, but to a change for the better in the life of humanity as a whole. His third dream concerned the political conditions for this change. Its realization would involve "an international unification of the separate existence of the peoples", a unity in diversity that would draw them together while "preserving and securing their national life". Thirty years earlier this dream had inspired his major work of political thought, *The Ideal of Human Unity*. Now, against all odds, the unification of humankind appeared to have begun. Though the United Nations was only "an imperfect initiative", the momentum was there "and, if the experience of history can be taken as a guide, it must inevitably increase until it conquers".[4]

Sri Aurobindo's last two dreams pertained more directly to the work in which he had been engaged since he came to Pondicherry. One of these was "the gift by India of her spiritual knowledge and her means for the spiritualisation of life to the whole race". The beginnings of this process could already be observed: "India's spirituality is entering Europe and America in an ever increasing measure. That movement will grow", he asserted. The last and boldest of his five dreams consisted of nothing less than "a new step in the evolution" which would begin to solve the perennial problems of human existence "by uplifting the consciousness to a higher level". Such an evolutionary leap forward appeared to be the most "impossible" of his dreams and the furthest from any prospect of fulfilment. It was still only "a personal hope and an idea and ideal which has begun to take hold both in India and in

---

4 Aurobindo 2006: 475-76.

the West on forward-looking minds". Yet the attempt to conceptualize it and to find the means to realize it is recognized as Sri Aurobindo's most distinctive philosophical and spiritual contribution. What he envisaged was not a technological transhumanism such as some futurists now theorize, but a suprarational transformation. He believed that here again the initiative could come from India, "although the scope must be universal".[5]

The juxtaposition of these two public statements by leading figures in modern Indian history, broadcast for the same epochal occasion, highlights the similarities and differences between two visions of India. Nehru and Sri Aurobindo agreed on the far-reaching importance of India's freedom and the possibilities it unleashed, not only for her own people but for the world. It might have seemed at the time as if both overestimated her future role. In 1947 many observers did not expect India to last long as a nation, much less as a democracy. Though the skeptics have been proved wrong, independent India remained for decades a poor "third world" country with little say in international affairs despite her huge population and the riches of her cultural heritage.

Over half a century after Independence, there is more reason to take seriously Sri Aurobindo's assurance that India will play a great part in humanity's future, as well as Nehru's declaration that India's tryst with destiny was also a fateful moment for Asia and the world. As the former UN diplomat Shashi Tharoor puts it with regard to India's place in international politics:

> We are now in a position to graduate from a focus on our own sovereign autonomy to exercising a vision of responsibility on the world stage, from a post-colonial concern with self-protection to a new role participating in

---

5 Aurobindo 2006: 475, 477.

the making of global rules and even playing a role in imposing them.[6]

The Statesman and the Sage

Nehru seems at first sight to diverge markedly from Sri Aurobindo on the question of the spiritual future of humanity and India's potential contribution to it. Yet the differences between the two in their attitudes toward religion and spirituality can easily be overstated by stereotyping both of these complex individuals. Misconceptions on this matter pertain not only to the perception of personalities, but to the larger issue of the relationship between secular and religious or spiritual values. That is a subject whose discussion often generates more heat than light. A nuanced understanding of the ideas of these leading Indian proponents of secular and spiritual viewpoints might help to clarify the alternatives.

A passage in Nehru's autobiography, written in prison in the 1930s, is representative of what he had to say about religion:

> India is supposed to be a religious country above everything else, and Hindu and Moslem and Sikh and others take pride in their faiths and testify to their truth by breaking heads. The spectacle of what is called religion, or at any rate organised religion, in India and elsewhere has filled me with horror, and I have frequently condemned it and wished to make a clean sweep of it. Almost always it seems to stand for blind belief and reaction, dogma and bigotry, superstition and exploitation, and the preservation of vested interests.[7]

If the passage had ended here, it would have situated the future prime minister solidly in the anti-religious camp and seemingly at the opposite pole from the sage of Pondicherry, whose words are often quoted by Hindu nationalists. But things are not so simple in either case. First of all, Nehru goes

[6] Tharoor 2013: 15.

[7] Nehru 1962: 374.

on to qualify his negative assessment of the role of religion in human life:

> And yet I knew well that there was something else in it, something which supplied a deep inner craving of human beings.

To be sure, the peace that religion has brought "to innumerable tortured souls" does not by itself prove that there is any truth in it. Perhaps religion only provides "the shelter of blind belief and absence of questioning, the calm that comes from being safe in harbour, protected from the storms of the open sea". Personally Nehru preferred "the open sea, with all its storms and tempests". But he could not deny that there might be something more to religion than "a safe anchorage from doubt and mental conflict". He even admitted: "In some cases certainly it was something more".[8]

"The usual religious outlook," Nehru complained, "is far removed from what I consider spirituality and things of the spirit, and it deliberately or unconsciously shuts its eyes to reality lest reality may not fit in with preconceived notions." This is hardly a repudiation of religion as such; the criticism of its "usual" forms is offset by the high value evidently placed on "spirituality and things of the spirit". Going to the heart of the question, Nehru wrote:

> What then is religion (to use the word in spite of its obvious disadvantages)? Probably it consists of the inner development of the individual, the evolution of his consciousness in a certain direction which is considered good. What that direction is will again be a matter for debate. But, as far as I understand it, religion lays stress on this inner change and considers outward change as but the projection of this inner development.[9]

---

[8] Nehru 1962: 374, 377.

[9] Ibid.: 377, 379.

Much of this statement could almost have been written by Sri Aurobindo. He, too, regarded true religion or spirituality as consisting of an inner development or evolution of the consciousness of the individual human being. As he wrote with regard to his own system of spiritual practice, it involves subtle, psychological processes of "working out by inner means the change of the consciousness. This does not mean that there is no outer change, – the outer change is necessary but as a part of the inner change."[10] There are significant differences, of course, between these two Cambridge-educated intellectuals even when their language is similar. Sri Aurobindo's utterances on spirituality, though far from dogmatic, have none of the tentativeness of Nehru's speculations. Rather than a few paragraphs of generalities, he wrote detailed expositions of this subject filling several volumes. Some would call it the difference between intellectual idealism and spiritual realization. However, we do not seem to be confronted with radically conflicting standpoints.

Nehru once wrote to Gandhi that religion was "not familiar ground" for him, but that he had "something else in its place" which gave him strength and hope. This was "something older than just intellect and reason", an "indefinable and indefinite urge, which may have just a tinge of religion in it and yet is wholly different from it".[11] These words, again, are not those of a diehard atheist. On the other hand, he could be scathingly critical of organized religion. But on this subject Sri Aurobindo was sometimes equally caustic, as when he remarked:

> Organised religion itself has often enough in the past hounded men to crime and massacre and justified obscurantism and oppression.[12]

---

10 Aurobindo 2014: 42.

11 Khilnani 2007: 89.

12 Aurobindo 1998a: 120.

Sri Aurobindo's impression of Nehru was that

> he bears on himself the stamp of a very fine character, a nature . . . full of rectitude and a high sense of honour: a man of the finest Brahmin type with what is best in European education added.

Asked about Nehru's spiritual possibilities, he observed privately in the same letter:

> For the spiritual life there is perhaps no immediate possibility: his mind stands in between, for it has seized strongly the Socialist dream of social perfection by *outward* change as the thing to be striven for and has made that into a sort of religion. The best possible on earth has been made by his mind its credo: the something beyond he does not believe in, the something more here would seem to him a dream without basis, I suppose.

Yet he concluded,

> He is a man with a strong psychic element and in this life or another that must go beyond the mind to find its source.[13]

Based on what he knew of Nehru's opinions, without having read his writings, Sri Aurobindo commented in another letter that he did "not take the same view of the Hindu religion as Jawaharlal". He went on to give his own evaluation of Hinduism:

> Religion is always imperfect because it is a mixture of man's spirituality with the errors that come in trying to sublimate ignorantly his lower nature. Hindu religion appears to me as a cathedral temple half in ruins, noble in the mass, often fantastic in detail, but always fantastic with a significance – crumbled and overgrown in many places, but a cathedral temple in which service is still done to the Unseen and its real presence can be felt by those who enter with the right spirit. The outer social structure which it built for its approach is another matter.[14]

---

13 Aurobindo 2011: 194. Italics in original.

14 Ibid.: 702-03.

We do not know what Nehru would have thought of this image purporting to describe a view different from his own. Sri Aurobindo's deep appreciation of the inner spirit of Hinduism is evident, but it is equally clear that he did not endorse every belief and practice associated with it. He stressed that his ashram – "so-called for want of a better word"[15] – had "nothing to do with Hindu religion or culture or any religion or nationality".[16] He even wrote on one occasion that he had "not the slightest objection to Hinduism being broken to pieces and disappearing from the face of the earth, if that is the Divine Will".[17] Nehru, too, was ambivalent about much of what survived of India's ancient traditions. In his last will and testament – where among other things he requested that, after his cremation, a handful of the ashes be thrown in the Gaṅgā – he spoke of his relationship to his country's past:

> And though I have discarded much of past tradition and custom, and am anxious that India should rid herself of all shackles that bind and constrain her and divide her people . . . I do not wish to cut myself off from the past completely. . . . I am conscious that I too, like all of us, am a link in that unbroken chain which goes back to the dawn of history in the immemorial past of India.[18]

An Elusive Unity

How was this chain of history to be kept unbroken, yet flexible enough to permit progress and transformation? In a more and more modernized and globalized world, how could a distinctively Indian civilizational sphere be preserved, not as a museum of cultural artifacts, but as a center of creativity and

[15] Aurobindo 2006: 441.

[16] Aurobindo 2011: 701.

[17] Ibid.

[18] Tharoor 2012: 186.

dynamism? Such questions preoccupied the thinkers and visionaries who led the nation to freedom. India's staggering diversity posed a related problem which all who worked for the country's independence had to face. As soon as they looked beyond the anti-colonial struggle to ponder what would happen once freedom was won, they were compelled to ask: when foreign rule ended, what would hold the new nation together?

As the political scientist Sunil Khilnani points out, by the 1920s at least three candidates for the unifying factor had been put forward:

> Nationalist Hindus asserted that Indian unity could be found in its common culture derived from religion; Gandhi, too, settled on religion as a source of interconnection among Indians, but manufactured his own eclectic and pluralist morality from different religious traditions; others, for whom Nehru became the most effective spokesman, turned away from religion and discovered a basis for unity both in a shared historical past of cultural mixing, and a future project of common development.[19]

To these could be added a fourth alternative. Sri Aurobindo discerned a spiritual as well as cultural basis for India's unity which differed from Gandhi's syncretic religiosity, but also had little in common with the homogeneity sought by Hindu nationalists. He did not minimize the problems created by "the centrifugal tendency of an extraordinary number and variety of disparate elements". But these only made India "an experiment of unparalleled complexity and potential richness", where all possible difficulties had been accumulated "in order to arrive at the most opulent result".[20]

Given the complexity of these cultural materials, the outcome of the Indian experiment could not easily be foreseen.

---

[19] Khilnani 1998: 154.

[20] Aurobindo 1998b: 16.

Welcoming the revitalization and "fresh self-affirmation" of "the old religious sects and disciplines", Sri Aurobindo noted approvingly that Islam, too, had "recently shared in the general stirring" and that there were "attempts to return vitally to the original Islamic ideals or to strike out fresh developments". But as for what would "finally come out of all this stir and ferment", he did not hazard a prediction:

> Perhaps none of these forms, nor all the sum of them may be definitive, they may constitute only the preparatory self-finding of the Indian spiritual mind recovering its past and turning towards its future.[21]

Sri Aurobindo's vision was characterized, as much as Nehru's, by an orientation toward the future much more than toward the past and by an acceptance of the inevitability and desirability of change.

Spiritual unity as Sri Aurobindo conceived it, unlike more external kinds of unity, was "a large and flexible thing" which "lives diffused in the system and permits readily a great diversity and freedom of life".[22] This idea of the spiritual oneness of India underlying its exuberant cultural and religious variety took pluralism for granted, but did not imply a Gandhian eclecticism or moralism. Among the other chief architects of Indian nationhood, it was Nehru who most vividly evoked a similar sense of this impalpable unity. Speaking of the "complex and mysterious personality of India", Nehru wrote:

> It was not her wide spaces that eluded me, or even her diversity, but some depth of soul which I could not fathom, though I had occasional and tantalizing glimpses of it. . . . Though outwardly there was diversity and infinite variety among our people, everywhere there was that tremendous

21 Aurobindo 2004: 25.

22 Ibid.: 431.

> impress of oneness, which had held all of us together for ages past, whatever political fate or misfortune had befallen us. The unity of India was no longer merely an intellectual conception for me: it was an emotional experience which overpowered me.

Intangible as this unity might seem, historically it "had been so powerful that no political division, no disaster or catastrophe, had been able to overcome it". This "spirit of India" was what Nehru sought as an inspiration for his political work, because "if we were going to build the house of India's future, . . . we would have to dig deep for the foundations".[23]

Hindu Nationalism and the Idea of India

Neither Nehru nor Sri Aurobindo regarded the religious heterogeneity of Indian civilization as a threat to the unity of the nation. As Nehru saw it, the problem was that

> in political matters, religion has been displaced by what is called communalism, a narrow group mentality basing itself on a religious community but in reality concerned with political power and patronage for the interested group.[24]

Sri Aurobindo considered India's religious diversity to be an asset. For him, as for Nehru, the problem was not religious plurality, but intolerance and the politicization of religious identities. While religion in the superficial sense on which communal identities are based could be divisive, spirituality was a deeper and, he believed, potentially stronger factor conducive to unity without requiring uniformity. But the dominance of a single religion was not an option. "The moulding of the whole type of the national being to suit the limited dogmas, forms, tenets of a particular religion," he maintained, "would be impossible, even if it were desirable, in a country

23 Nehru 2010: 51-52.

24 Ibid.: 420.

full of the most diverse religious opinions and harbouring too three such distinct general forms as Hinduism, Islam and Christianity, to say nothing of the numerous special forms to which each of these has given birth. Spirituality is much wider than any particular religion."[25]

Those who are familiar with such passages in Sri Aurobindo's writings, but less acquainted with the Indian political and academic scenes, may be surprised to learn that in some circles in his own country he is routinely associated with the politico-religious ideology of Hindutva. Statements such as his assertion that he did "not understand Hindu nationalism as a possibility under modern conditions"[26] have been ignored by both proponents and opponents of Hindu nationalism, who for different reasons have found it useful for their own projects to identify him with a movement he rejected. "The mis-appropriation of Aurobindo by the Hindu right," remarks Harvard historian Sugata Bose, "has been facilitated by the secularists' abandonment of the domain of religion to the religious bigots." As a result, Sri Aurobindo has been mistaken for a "harbinger of communalism" by many secularist historians. "Indian intellectual history," Bose concludes, "needs to be rescued from this impoverished state."[27]

The current academic situation in India, in this regard, can be illustrated by the chapter on Sri Aurobindo in Jyotirmaya Sharma's *Hindutva*. Full of zeal "to confront Hindutva and its demonic agenda," Sharma sets out to "call the bluff of a set of self-appointed arbiters of faith." He takes Aurobindo to be one of these, deeming him second to none in his contribution to the rise of the "terrible and tortured vision" of Hindutva. Near the end of the chapter he makes some startling claims:

---

25 Aurobindo 2004: 33.

26 Aurobindo 1997d: 304.

27 Bose 2013: 112-13.

> By 1939, Aurobindo's utterances on Hinduism and Hindus seemed to echo the notions of Hindutva that Savarkar was advocating. Absent was any idea of a liberal democratic nation, based on an impersonal and formal notion of rule of law, respect for plurality and ensuring a minimum amount of liberty for all. Rather, it was a war of incommensurable ideas of identity politics masquerading as rival notions of morality.[28]

Vinayak Damodar Savarkar's attitude toward Islam, as Sharma points out in a later chapter, "remained unchanged from the time he pelted stones on a mosque in Bhagur as a twelve-year-old".[29] Aurobindo as caricatured by Sharma hardly differs from Savarkar, except that his imagined conversion to Hindu fanaticism and Islamophobia is supposed to have occurred only in his later years.

Sharma concedes:

> As a revolutionary nationalist writing in the first decade of the twentieth century, Aurobindo welcomed Pan-Islamism and the rise of a separate Muslim self-consciousness. He saw it as a sign of the vitality of nationalism and as part of the process of nation building. Nevertheless, he opposed the idea of separate electorates for Hindus and Muslims because this concept recognized both communities as permanently separate political units.[30]

This is one of Sharma's rare gestures toward a balanced interpretation which eludes him in the end. In fact, concern about the danger of policies that could foster communalism was a consistent feature of Sri Aurobindo's thinking on Hindu–Muslim relations whenever he turned his attention to them. In 1936 he wrote:

---

28 Sharma 2003: 13, 8, 69.

29 Ibid.: 133.

30 Ibid.: 64.

> What has created the Hindu-Moslem split was . . . the acceptance of the communal principle by the Congress. . . . The recognition of that communal principle at Lucknow made them [the Muslims] permanently a separate *political* entity in India which ought never to have happened.[31]

This view of the Lucknow Pact of December 1916 is shared by liberal Muslims such as the historian Mushirul Hasan. Commenting on the endorsement of the Lucknow Pact by both "Hindu publicists" and secularists in the Congress party, Hasan observes:

> In this way both groups legitimised – each in its own independent perspective – the gradual evolution of a *Muslim* personality in Indian politics. In so doing they . . . aided a potentially divisive trend. . . . The energy derived from recognising Muslims as a distinct religious and political unit implied that the basic terms of reference precluded any lasting solution of the communal tangle.[32]

Sharma acknowledges that Aurobindo opposed, while he was politically active, the effort of the Hindu Sabha to unite Hindus against Muslims. But he goes on to claim that Aurobindo's attitude toward Muslims became more and more antagonistic after he left politics in 1910. By 1939, in Sharma's creative retelling of intellectual history, the revolutionary turned Maharṣi had become "a pamphleteer of the Hindu *rashtra* concept without being conscious of it".[33]

In 1939-40 Sri Aurobindo was occupied with the revision of his monumental philosophical work, *The Life Divine*, where the words "Hindu" and "Hinduism" do not occur. When he speaks there of "religion in India", he does not limit it to Hinduism or even to religions of Indian origin. In India, he

---

31 Aurobindo 2011: 21. Italics in original.

32 Hasan 1997: 50. Italics in original.

33 Sharma 2003: 69.

writes, religion "admitted a vast number of different formulations". He continues:

> Its method has been . . . to follow every possible way of advance to the goal and test it even to its extreme. . . . Even the exclusive credal type of religion was not itself excluded; provided its affinity to the general aim and principle was clear, it was admitted into the infinite variety of the general order.[34]

In another writing Sri Aurobindo contrasts the "religious culture which now goes by the name of Hinduism" with "certain credal religions", probably alluding to those of the Semitic kind.[35] In *The Life Divine*, however, these religions as practiced in India are also subsumed under the broad phenomenon of Indian religion, to whose "infinite variety" they contribute. There is nothing here that suggests any affinity, conscious or otherwise, with the concept of a Hindu *rāṣṭra* (kingdom) as alleged by Sharma.

Throughout the period when Sharma is convinced that Aurobindo was preoccupied "more than ever before" by the "Hindu–Muslim question",[36] his voluminous writings contain only a few brief references to this question. Sharma does not quote them, but they do not support his conclusions. So what is he talking about? His contention that there was a "shift" toward intolerance in Aurobindo's attitude toward Muslims after 1910 is based on a few quotations from two sections of a recent book, compiled anonymously and published in Paris, entitled *India's Rebirth*. These sections consist not of writings by Sri Aurobindo, but of reports of conversations with him whose substance was later jotted down from memory by a participant. Most of the reported conversations first appeared, scattered among discussions of many unrelated topics, in three

---

34 Aurobindo 2005a: 904-06.

35 Aurobindo 2004: 179.

36 Sharma 2003: 67.

volumes entitled *Evening Talks with Sri Aurobindo*, published between 1959 and 1966.

Evening Talks were recorded by A.B. Purani, who left the freedom struggle in Gujarat to come to Pondicherry in the year when the first series of talks began. It is anyone's guess how much his recently renounced activism, at a time when the Hindu–Muslim rift was widening, might have colored his recollections of what was said on that subject. In any case, he preceded his version of the conversations with a note explaining that Sri Aurobindo was "not responsible for these records as he had no opportunity to see them". It was "not as if Sri Aurobindo said exactly these things," Purani clarified, "but that I remember him to have said them". In his introduction, he added that what was said in this small group "was not intended by Sri Aurobindo to be the independent expression of his views on the subjects, events or the persons discussed" and that the talks "were not intended by him to be noted down".[37]

Sharma thinks that "Aurobindo moved close to issuing the Muslims a warning"[38] in 1923 through a remark attributed to him in one of these informal, posthumously published talks. We do not know what Sri Aurobindo actually said on this occasion. What we do know is that when a correspondent asked him in 1932 if there was "any likelihood of a fight between the Hindus and Mahomedans in India," he replied: "If they fight, neither are likely to gain but both to lose".[39] If this was a warning, it was directed equally to Hindus and Muslims.

Purani's version of a conversation of 1939, after a gap in the talks since 1926, prompts Sharma to depict Aurobindo as a propagandist for a Hindu state, whose "writings . . . have

---

37 Purani 2007: 9, 11.

38 Sharma 2003: 67.

39 Aurobindo 2011: 697.

inspired a jihadi Hinduism".[40] By "writings" he evidently means the *Evening Talks*, since he quotes nothing else to support this part of his argument. It is implied that the statements he cites as Aurobindo's, or similar ones by him, played a role in whipping up the frenzy which led to events such as the demolition of the Babri Masjid in 1992. He does not explain how this could have happened. It is doubtful whether Sharma himself would have located these little-known materials if they had not been collected in *India's Rebirth*, the source he gives in his references. That compilation was first published *after* Ayodhya.

The historian Peter Heehs has surveyed the work of scholars who perpetuate an unexamined "historiographical commonplace" about Aurobindo, portraying him as a religious politician who contributed to the rise of communalism in India. He comments:

> Unable to come up with a convincing historical, sociological, or psychological explanation of the phenomenon of communalism, they identify Aurobindo – a name, an ascribed opinion, a stray quotation – as one of the causes of the problem. . . . He is treated as a symbolic icon, a whipping-boy rather than a complex human being. The vicarious punishment he and others have to bear does not go far in finding a solution, but it at least makes his secular detractors feel better.[41]

Jyotirmaya Sharma exemplifies this approach. His manner of dealing with the post-revolutionary Aurobindo is rhetorical rather than analytical. He quotes snippets of conversation, reported from memory and compiled several decades later, instead of examining authentic works of social and political thought published by the author. Even these snippets he reads anachronistically, seeing them neither in the context of the anti-colonial movement nor in relation to the development of

---

40 Sharma 2003: 69.

41 Heehs 2006: 152.

Aurobindo's thought, but in the distorting mirror of recent events and altered circumstances. Sharma had little reason to worry that his methods would be criticized. He could safely assume that few in his academic audience would question the familiar stereotype he was recycling.

Nevertheless this stereotype can and should be challenged, not only for the sake of an accurate assessment of Sri Aurobindo as an individual thinker, but to retrieve the vision of India he represents. This was not a purely political construct, but neither was it a narrowly religious conception. Like Nehru, Aurobindo sought the "spirit of India" in a "depth of soul" he tried to fathom. He perceived this "group-soul" to be a unifying, but not homogenizing, factor. On the contrary, it "works out its tendencies by a diversity of opinions, a diversity of wills, a diversity of life, and the vitality of the group-life depends largely upon the working of this diversity, its continuity, its richness".[42]

The Meeting-Place of Religions

At the Parliament of Religions in Chicago in 1893, Swami Vivekananda introduced himself as belonging "to a nation which has sheltered the persecuted and the refugees of all religions".[43] He alluded to the Cochin Jews and to the Indian Zoroastrians or Parsis. He could have added the Syrian Christians. These communities were well-established in India by the end of the first millennium CE. Islam arrived under different circumstances; but as Sri Aurobindo points out, Muslim domination "ceased very rapidly to be a foreign rule"[44] and Muslims in India today "belong as much to the Indian nation as the Hindus themselves".[45] The same is true of

---

42 Aurobindo 1998a: 210.

43 Barrows 1893, vol. 1: 102.

44 Aurobindo 2004: 441.

45 Aurobindo 2006: 104.

Christians descended from colonial-era converts. Then there are the indigenous religions, some of considerable antiquity such as Jainism. The syncretic Sikh religion stands in a class by itself. All this and more adds up to an astonishing multireligious assemblage, whose relatively peaceful continuation for many centuries has no parallel in human history.

"India is the meeting-place of the religions", Sri Aurobindo observed. Hinduism itself, though usually counted as only one of these, was "a vast and complex thing, not so much a religion as a great diversified and yet subtly unified mass of spiritual thought, realisation and aspiration".[46] There was no reason to want to abrogate all this diversity. "The coming of so many religions to India," Sri Aurobindo insisted, "was part of her spiritual destiny and a great advantage for the work to be done".[47] But certain unresolved tensions could not be denied. The most acute dated back to the time of the Muslim conquest of much of the mainly Hindu subcontinent.

The problem was due to "the struggle between two civilisations, one ancient and indigenous, the other mediaeval and brought in from outside", each attached to a powerful religion. There seemed to be two conceivable solutions, one political and secular, the other spiritual but not based on any single religion. The first possibility was "a political patriotism surmounting the religious struggle and uniting the two communities". The second was "the rise of a greater spiritual principle and formation which could reconcile the two".[48] During the last few centuries both approaches have been tried, but the problem has yet to be solved.

As a nationalist leader, Sri Aurobindo hoped that the patriotism aroused by the struggle for freedom would be

---

46 Aurobindo 2004: 25.

47 Aurobindo 2011: 700.

48 Aurobindo 2004: 442.

enough to bring Hindus and Muslims together in a feeling of common nationhood. In later writings he called such patriotism the "religion of country". This was not religion in the usual sense, though it may adopt similar symbols. He defined it as

> a constant even if not always explicit recognition not only of the sacredness of the physical mother, the land, but also, in however obscure a way, of the nation as a collective soul.[49]

After his withdrawal from politics, the scope of Sri Aurobindo's political thought broadened. No longer focusing on nationalism and the religion of country, he dwelt increasingly on internationalism and the religion of humanity. However, he saw no conflict between the two. From the beginning, his nationalism had been in the liberal tradition referred to by the political theorist Benjamin Barber:

> Liberal and romantic nationalists from Herder to Mazzini subscribed at once to a religion of humanity deifying a single, cosmopolitan conception of human nature *and* a vigorous nationality: in Mazzini's arching rhetoric "nationality is the role assigned by God to each people in the work of humanity."[50]

An expression of Indian patriotism that Sri Aurobindo endorsed, even long after his days in the freedom struggle, was the use of Bankim Chandra Chatterjee's poem "Vande Mataram" as a national song. In 1939, told of the proposed deletion of an allusion to the goddess Durgā to avoid offending Muslims, he reportedly said:

> But it is not a religious song! It is a national song and the Durga spoken of is India as the Mother. Why shouldn't the Muslims accept it? It is an image used in poetry.[51]

---

49 Aurobindo 1998b: 292.

50 Barber 1996: 159. Italics in original.

51 Purani 2007: 717.

In another conversation on this subject, earlier the same year, he seems to have replied similarly:

> But here the country is spoken of as "Durga", so a Hindu goddess has nothing to do with it.

Otherwise, he added, Christians might as well object to the representation of Greek gods and goddesses in literature.[52] Nationalism, like literature, transcended for him the narrowness of religious orthodoxy.

"Vande Mataram," observes the political philosopher Martha Nussbaum, "as championed and interpreted by the Hindu nationalist movement . . . expresses a conception of Indian identity . . . that seems at least potentially exclusionary." She adds, however:

> The song itself is a beautiful poem that can be read innocuously, as it was by philosopher Sri Aurobindo when he translated it into English.[53]

Unlike Nussbaum, Jyotirmaya Sharma thinks the song to be inescapably exclusionary and Aurobindo's approval of it tantamount to a declaration of war on non-Hindus.[54] But this interpretation overlooks, among other things, the secular reasoning behind Sri Aurobindo's position. When he described "Vande Mataram" as a literary and patriotic rather than a religious poem, he was rejecting identity politics and pointing

---

52 Nirodbaran 2001: 246. Nirodbaran, a participant in the series of talks with Sri Aurobindo that began in December 1938, recorded some of the same talks as Purani during this period. However, the two talks on "Vande Mataram" in October and December 1939 are not among those for which two versions are available. A comparison of Purani's and Nirodbaran's versions of talks recorded by both shows similarities and differences which give an idea of the imperfect reliability of their reports.

53 Nussbaum 2007: 11-12.

54 Sharma 2003: 68-69.

out the artificiality of supposed obstacles to a nationalism in which Hindus, Muslims and others could participate equally. His view on this minor question has to be seen in the larger perspective of his political thought and its underlying philosophy. So understood, it reflects a distinctive approach to religious and cultural differences which could contribute, especially in India, to discussions of what we now call pluralism and multiculturalism.

Interconnected Differences

The Republic of India was founded as an experiment in multicultural democracy, arguably the largest, earliest and most hazardous such experiment ever attempted. Multiculturalism as it is understood today is a recent development. Canadian political philosopher Will Kymlicka speaks of "a veritable revolution around the world in the relations between states and ethnocultural minorities" since the late 1960s. Around then, "models of assimilationist and homogenizing nation-states" began to be replaced by "newer 'multicultural' models of the state and of citizenship".[55] But in India, the older models had been rejected two decades earlier in favor of what was at that time an almost untried alternative. Sunil Khilnani compares the challenges that faced the fathers of Indian democracy with the simpler experience of most other nations.

> There were few models, from either European or any other history, that could be used to help focus India's assorted diversities into a political structure founded upon a democratic principle. This had to be invented through practice.... The multiplicity of cultural and political voices in the society demanded recognition. No attempt was made to impose a single or uniform 'Indian' identity upon the new nation. This, seen as a potential weakness from the perspective of the Western theories of nationalism which

[55] Kymlicka 2007: 3.

> guided the thinking of nationalist Hindus, was actually the most remarkable achievement.[56]

Khilnani gives much of the credit for this to Nehru, who managed to avoid two extremes in the handling of cultural variety. At the liberal extreme, individual rationality is understood to be essentially unconstrained by cultural heritage. This leaves little room for multicultural policies, whose stress on group identities may conflict with personal freedom. At the other pole, cultures are regarded as separate, internally homogeneous entities severely limiting the options available to the individuals that constitute them. This conception can be applied in two contrasting ways. Ethnic nationalism invokes it conservatively to justify putting the state in the hands of a single dominant community. This is the antithesis of multiculturalism. But it is also possible, as Khilnani observes, to take "a more benign view of the state as curator of cultural exhibits, responsible for protecting and preserving communities".[57] The implementations of multiculturalism in a number of countries in the last few decades would fit this description.

Nehru himself was a liberal cosmopolitan. While this did not stop him from appreciating India's profusion of cultural traditions, he never took them to be incapable of progressive change or creative interaction. As Khilnani puts it, he came to see "cultures as overlapping forms of activity that had commerce with one another, mutually altering and reshaping each other". In sum, India as Nehru envisioned it "was a society neither of liberal individuals nor of exclusive communities or nationalities, but of interconnected differences".[58]

In a European context, the British-Indian political philosopher Bhikhu Parekh advocates "a transformative and

---

56 Khilnani 1998: 172-73.

57 Khilnani 1998: 171.

58 Ibid.: 171-72.

open-minded dialogue" among people of different cultures and religions, as opposed to "a narrow and static view of multiculturalism" leading to "a compartmentalised social and cultural universe".[59] Such a dialogic approach is now sometimes called interculturalism. Nehru in his own way seems to have intuitively anticipated this recent development in multicultural theory, applying it as far as circumstances permitted in the first two decades of India's existence as a democracy.

Orthodoxy and the God Within

Like Nehru, Sri Aurobindo was keenly aware of India's myriad cultural and religious divisions, but did not take them to be unalterable or unbridgeable. He also shared with Nehru the hope that India would not cling unduly to the mixed legacy of the past, but turn increasingly toward the incalculable possibilities of the future. He differed from Nehru in assigning a key role to spirituality in the kind of future he envisaged. This has been interpreted as a Hindu vision. But that interpretation can be supported, if at all, only by statements found in his early writings and speeches, such as those published in 1909-10 in the weekly journal *Karmayogin*. He later distanced himself from the writings of that period, remarking in 1937:

> My spiritual consciousness and knowledge at that time was as nothing to what it is now – how would the change leave my view of politics and life unmodified altogether?[60]

Sri Aurobindo's own ashram was, he clarified, "not a religious association. Those who are here come from all religions and some are of no religion."[61] The majority of its members, it is true, came from Hindu backgrounds. Partly for this reason and because his writings include commentaries on Sanskrit

---

59 Parekh 2008: 30.

60 Aurobindo 2011: 77.

61 Aurobindo 2006: 531.

texts usually considered to be scriptures of Hinduism, Sri Aurobindo is often assumed to have been a Hindu teacher. That is not how he identified himself, however. He developed an original philosophy and a method of spiritual practice which, whatever features they may have in common with certain Hindu traditions, were clearly distinguished by him from any form of Hinduism. He explained to a Muslim in the ashram:

> As for giving up one's past, if that means giving up the outer forms of the old religions, it is done as much by the Hindus here as by the Mahomedans. . . . What is kept of Hinduism is Vedanta and Yoga, in which Hinduism is one with Sufism of Islam and with the Christian mystics. But even here it is not Vedanta and Yoga in their traditional limits (their past), but widened and rid of many ideas that are peculiar to the Hindus. If I have used Sanskrit terms and figures, it is because I know them and do not know Persian and Arabic. I have not the slightest objection to anyone here drawing inspiration from Islamic sources.[62]

This was written with reference to the small nucleus of seekers that had gathered around Sri Aurobindo in Pondicherry. But since he regarded his ashram as a kind of laboratory for experimenting with possibilities of self-transformation, it is also relevant to grasping the nature of the spiritual principle he proposed as a basis for reconciling India's religious communities if the unifying power of patriotism proved insufficient. The mention of Sufism in the above letter suggests what he had in mind.

Sufism, as the Scottish historian William Dalrymple points out, "has always borne remarkable similarities to certain currents in Hindu mysticism". Dalrymple goes on to indicate how the reconciliation of Islam and Hinduism can be, and has been, approached from the Muslim side:

---

62 Aurobindo 2011: 700-01.

> The Sufis believed that this search for God within and the quest for *fana* – total immersion in the absolute – liberated the seeker from the restrictions of narrow orthodoxy, allowing the devotee to look beyond the letter of the law to its mystical essence. This allowed the Sufis for the first time to bring together Hindu and Muslim in an accessible and popular movement which spanned the apparently unbridgeable gulf separating the two religions. The teachings of Sufi poetry and song also provided a link between the devotions of the villagers and the high philosophical subtleties of the mystics.[63]

As far as the Sufis Dalrymple met in Sindh were concerned,

> it was not they who were the heretics, so much as the stern Wahhabi mullahs who criticized the popular Islam of the Sufi saints as *shirk*, or heresy: "These mullahs are just hypocrites," said one old fakir I talked to in the shrine. "Without love, they distort the true meaning of the teaching of the Prophet."[64]

Mysticism offers one way of reducing the gap between religious world-views. The growth of a more secular and rational outlook offers another. In either case, orthodoxy is the obstacle. Sri Aurobindo warned against attachment to a conservative religious mentality:

> There is no place for rigid orthodoxy, whether Hindu, Mahomedan or Christian in the future. Those who cling to it, lose hold on life and go under – as has been shown by the fate of the Hindus in India and of the orthodox Mahomedan countries all over the world. It is only where there has been an opening to new light and inevitable change that strength is returning as in Turkey and Persia.[65]

---

63 Dalrymple 2011: 110.

64 Ibid.: 112.

65 Aurobindo 2011: 697-98.

This stricture applies to all religions. Jyotirmaya Sharma paraphrases Sri Aurobindo as saying that Islam in India was in need of a movement that would remodel the religion and change the Muslim temperament.[66] Supposing it to have been accurately reported, this statement has to be understood in relation to others which insist on the need for a transformation not only in Islam but in all religions, including Hinduism.

Tolerance in a Multireligious Society

Sharma objects to a remark ascribed to Sri Aurobindo to the effect that tensions between Hindus and Muslims can be resolved only if Muslims learn tolerance.[67] This comment, if it was made, may seem one-sided today when Hindus do not have a much better reputation for tolerance than Muslims. But the rise of Hindu militancy since the late 1980s has taken many observers by surprise. French political scientist Christophe Jaffrelot points out that "the establishment and later expansion of the militant Hindu movement are indeed modern phenomena which took place despite the original characteristics of Hinduism". These characteristics included "a socio-cultural differentiation and a capacity for integration which hardly seem compatible with the expression of a militant collective consciousness".[68] The notion of the mild and tolerant Hindu may now look like an exploded myth, but it had a historical basis and was long accepted even by many people who were not admirers of Hinduism.

Sri Aurobindo usually took the idea of Hindu tolerance for granted, though he recognized past episodes in India of "mutual hatred and occasional though brief-lived persecution of Buddhist, Jain, Shaiva, Vaishnava".[69] With regard to Islam,

---

66 Sharma 2003: 68. Cf. Purani 2007: 267.

67 Ibid.; ibid.: 295.

68 Jaffrelot 1996: 1, 5.

69 Aurobindo 1998a: 176.

he is recorded as saying in another discussion cited by Sharma:

> You can live amicably with a religion whose principle is toleration. But how is it possible to live peacefully with a religion whose principle is "I will not tolerate you"?[70]

Sharma reads this as an example of Hindu intolerance and proof of Aurobindo's Islamophobia. But two observations need to be made. First, it should hardly need to be reiterated that the report of any such unverifiable remark cannot be given the same weight as the view of Islam that emerges from Sri Aurobindo's undeniably authentic writings. These present a broadly favorable picture of the religion. His appreciation of Moghul tolerance is highlighted by the economist and Nobel laureate Amartya Sen, who notes:

> The exponents of contemporary Hindu politics in India often try to deny the tolerant nature of much of Moghul rule. That tolerance was, however, handsomely acknowledged by Hindu leaders of an earlier vintage. For example, Sri Aurobindo, who established the famous ashram in Pondicherry, specifically identified this aspect of the Moghul rule.[71]

Sen quotes Sri Aurobindo's assertion that the Moghul Empire was "more liberal and tolerant in religion than any mediaeval or contemporary [i.e., early modern] European kingdom or empire".[72] This statement occurs in a series of essays first published in 1920-21 and reprinted in 1947 in a booklet entitled *The Spirit and Form of Indian Polity*. It reliably represents Sri Aurobindo's settled and public view of the role of Islam in Indian history, unlike the sources used by Sharma to create the opposite impression.

---

70 Purani 2007: 303. Sharma (2003: 67) erroneously gives the date as 1909 instead of 1923.

71 Sen 1997: 25.

72 Aurobindo 2004: 443.

Muhammad himself is upheld by Sri Aurobindo as a supreme exemplar of the egoless Karmayogi, a channel of divine power through whom is accomplished a tremendous work for the world.[73] The Qur'an was "dictated to him often in a state of trance, in which he passed from his conscient into his superconscient self, by the Divinity to his secret intuitive mind".[74] As for Muslim zealots, Sri Aurobindo agreed with their moderate coreligionists that the fanatics "do and say extravagant things" in the name of Islam "which are not Islamic but a caricature of Islamic faith and action".[75]

The second observation regarding Sri Aurobindo's alleged remark on intolerance is more general. Sharma treats his reported query ("But how is it possible to live peacefully with a religion whose principle is 'I will not tolerate you'?") as an anti-Islamic provocation. But the problem of intolerance in multireligious societies is not solved by making discussion of it taboo for the sake of political correctness. No religion is inherently intolerant, but every religion is potentially so. Many scholars of religion would agree that this potential has been especially pronounced in monotheistic faiths, as well as in religious groups whose reaction to modernity has taken the form of fundamentalism (though the applicability of this term is disputed). Sharma misses the genuine issues involved here, including complex questions about religious exclusivism and identity politics in a global age. These issues are best examined in relation to ongoing debates on multiculturalism.

The German philosopher Jürgen Habermas points out the difficulty under present circumstances with "interpretations of the world that claim exclusiveness for a privileged way of life":

---

73 Aurobindo 1999: 253.

74 Aurobindo 1998b: 177.

75 Aurobindo 2012: 110.

> As the Rushdie case reminded us, a fundamentalism that leads to a practice of intolerance is incompatible with the democratic constitutional state. . . . Fundamentalist world-views . . . leave no room for reflection on their relationship with the other world-views with which they share the same universe of discourse. . . . They leave no room for "reasonable disagreement".

Coexistence in multicultural societies, Habermas maintains, requires "the mutual recognition of the different cultural memberships".[76] Some such requirement is presumably what Sri Aurobindo was alluding to when he reportedly commented on the difficulty of living with intolerance. His previously quoted admonition against "rigid orthodoxy" ("those who cling to it, lose hold on life and go under") and his insistence on "inevitable change"[77] also agree with the outlook expressed by Habermas, who writes: "The accelerated pace of change in modern societies explodes all stationary forms of life".[78] Under these conditions, exclusivism in the name of tradition cannot expect to be treated as sacrosanct. Religions undercut their own prospects of survival if they reject the ground rules needed for living side by side on this crowded and endangered planet. Nehru pointed out:

> The necessities of today will force us to formulate a new morality in accordance with them. If we are to find a way out of this crisis of the spirit and realise what are the true spiritual values today, we shall have to face the issues frankly and boldly and not take refuge under the dogmas of any religion.[79]

Liberalism subverts itself if it fosters illiberalism in its midst. The attitudes of majorities and minorities alike must change in order to adapt to each other. Bhikhu Parekh proposes an

---

76 Habermas 1994: 132-33.

77 Aurobindo 2011: 697.

78 Habermas 1994: 132.

79 Nehru 1962: 550.

"appeal to mutual cultural respect" as an approach to solving the "Muslim question" in Europe. He considers it "perfectly valid for the two parties to say that one of them cannot be expected to respect the deeply held cultural beliefs and practices of the other unless the latter does the same".[80] Ideally, Muslims should be reassured "that their culture is valued by the wider society". The wider society should also be reassured

> that it remains in charge of its cultural life, that Muslims will not seek to undermine it by irresponsible demands, and that the differences between the two are to be resolved through a rational dialogue conducted in a spirit of mutual commitment to a common life.[81]

In the West as well as in India, home of the world's largest Muslim minority, both sides have often had trouble fulfilling these conditions of mutual recognition. The relatively recent attempt of the "wider society" in Western countries to do so has been called multiculturalism. In India, the corresponding attempt goes under the name of secularism in the sense of state protection for all religions. These efforts have sometimes had unintended consequences. The attitudes and policies associated with multiculturalism, acknowledges the Indian-born English writer Kenan Malik, "have come to be regarded as the hallmarks of a progressive, anti-racist outlook and as the foundation stones of modern liberal democracies". Yet multiculturalism in Britain, he avers, has in practice "helped foster a more tribal nation and, within Muslim communities, has undermined progressive trends while strengthening the hand of conservative religious leaders". Liberals, he complains, have ignored the diversity in Muslim communities. Abandoning Enlightenment values, they have inadvertently

> helped build a culture of grievance in which being offended has become a badge of identity, cleared a space for radical

80 Parekh 2008: 27.

81 Ibid.: 26.

Islamists to flourish, and made secular and progressive arguments less sayable, particularly within Muslim communities.[82]

Enlightenment Values and Asian Civilizations

If liberal multiculturalists can be charged with betraying Enlightenment values, it is because those values themselves do not provide unambiguous solutions to today's dilemmas. The social and political ideals born of the Age of Enlightenment in seventeenth- and eighteenth-century Europe are encapsulated in the motto of the French revolution: *Liberté, Egalité, Fraternité*. But in practice, these ideals often conflict with each other. Each seems to point society and government in a somewhat different direction. At the root of the problem is the tension between the demands of the individual and the claims of the community. Liberty is the most individualistic principle, fraternity the most communitarian. "Liberty and fraternity were brother constructs of the French revolution," Benjamin Barber observes, "but like Cain and Abel were born to strife. Embeddedness means . . . membership in entities that constrain choice."[83]

Equality has an individualistic aspect, like liberty, but when understood collectively draws closer to fraternity. Multiculturalism takes the group as the unit with the aim of realizing equality in the increasingly diverse societies produced by globalization. But the policy of protecting rather than assimilating minority cultures tends to reinforce the solidarity of the group. By so doing, it can trap people in roles they might prefer to shed. Individual liberty may suffer for the sake of collective equality and communal cohesion. A commitment to the equality of groups distinguished by culture implies a pluralism that values diversity. But diversity can be understood

82 Malik 2009: xx, 210.

83 Barber 1996: 160-61.

in various ways and valued for a number of reasons. The stress may be on the group or the individual, identity or choice, preservation or progress, purity or hybridity, cultural boundaries or cross-cultural interaction. Differing combinations of emphasis produce a wide range of options.

The kind of equality that fosters diversity need not depend on ignoring all distinctions of relative value. Multicultural thinking often assumes that each culture not only gives meaning to the lives of those who participate in it, but has something significant to offer to the rest of humanity. This "presumption of worth", as the Canadian philosopher Charles Taylor calls it, "imagines a universe in which different cultures complement each other with quite different kinds of contribution". Assuming the differences to be non-trivial, therefore, the egalitarian outlook of multiculturalism has to be qualified; otherwise the celebration of diversity could end up being paradoxically homogenizing. Taylor explains:

> If all cultures have made a contribution of worth, it cannot be that these are identical, or even embody the same kind of worth. . . . This picture not only is compatible with, but demands judgments of, superiority-in-a-certain-respect.[84]

What this picture is incompatible with is any particular culture's claim to overall superiority and universality. The collapse of imperialism has discredited racial and cultural justifications of outright Western supremacy, though much Eurocentrism persists in subtler forms. But the horizons of Western thought had already begun to expand during the Renaissance. Some Enlightenment thinkers, and a few even earlier, cultivated an informed appreciation of distant cultures. At first China was the object of particular admiration. As the intellectual historian J.J. Clarke points out, the seventeenth-century French philosopher Pierre Bayle invoked the Chinese tradition of

---

[84] Taylor 1994: 71.

toleration "to attack religious intolerance and persecution at home". The best-known sinophile of the eighteenth century was Voltaire, who wrote a history of the world with chapters on several non-European countries in order to show that there were civilizations outside of Europe at least equal to the West in their cultural achievements. "This is an attitude," Clarke remarks, "which even in our own supposedly more enlightened times cannot be taken for granted."[85]

Western universalism is commonly justified by the argument that only values derived from the European Enlightenment can save the world from the ills of medievalism. But the claim that these enlightened values are uniquely Western as well as modern has been challenged. Amartya Sen comments on this claim with regard to the values assumed by the concept of human rights:

> The view that the basic ideas underlying freedom and rights in a tolerant society are "Western" notions, and somehow alien to Asia, is hard to make any sense of, even though that view has been championed by both Asian authoritarians and Western chauvinists.[86]

Sen agrees with Isaiah Berlin that "the comprehensive notion that makes up the contemporary idea of individual liberty as an entitlement of everyone"[87] is modern and was never clearly formulated in antiquity. But he believes that separate components of it were present as much in non-Western cultures as in the Greco-Roman world or in Christianity. In the West, an earnest if not altogether consistent attempt to put this idea into practice has been made only since the end of colonialism in the aftermath of the Second World War; until then, liberties were massively denied to subject peoples throughout the non-Western world. The elevation of this concept of freedom to a

85 Clarke 1997: 44, 46.

86 Sen 1997: 27.

87 Ibid.: 16.

would-be universal principle of modern life has coincided with the advent of the global age. The change has by no means occurred only in the West and there is no good reason to interpret its manifestations elsewhere as signs of Westernization.

In the West the spread of the ideal of religious tolerance can be traced to the Enlightenment. In most of Europe – with exceptions in Andalusia and later the Netherlands – it had been conspicuous by its absence until around the time when the English philosopher John Locke made his famous plea for it in 1689. Tolerance can hardly be called a distinctively Western virtue. The strong formulation it has been given in the modern West has been largely a reaction to the appalling record of intolerance that had previously marred so much of European history. In contrast, as Nehru observes in connection with the framing of a democratic constitution for India,

> the whole history of India was witness to the toleration and even encouragement of minorities and of different racial groups. There is nothing in Indian history to compare with the bitter religious feuds and persecutions that prevailed in Europe. So we did not have to go abroad for ideas of religious and cultural toleration; these were inherent in Indian life.[88]

Long before the French revolution, liberty, equality and fraternity were not unheard-of concepts even in lands far from Europe. "Equality and brotherhood in the faith," Sri Aurobindo notes, formed the "dominant principle" of Islamic civilization, where nothing prevented a slave "from rising even to the throne".[89] Likewise, Swami Vivekananda held that the "peculiar excellence" of Islam was that it "makes its followers all equal". What it came "to preach to the world is this practical brotherhood of all belonging to their faith".[90] Hinduism,

---

88 Nehru 2010: 420.

89 Aurobindo 1998b: 105.

90 Vivekananda 1989, vol. 2: 371.

especially in its Vedantic forms, excelled in showing the paths to spiritual liberation and taught an inner equality and unity. But it needed to learn something from Islam about the social application of these realizations, Vivekananda thought. In a letter quoted appreciatively by Nehru, he wrote to a Muslim friend that "practical Advaitism, which looks upon and behaves to all mankind as one's own soul, is yet to be developed among the Hindus universally". On the other hand, "if ever the followers of any religion approach to this equality in an appreciable degree in the plane of practical work-a-day life . . . it is those of Islam and Islam alone."[91]

Secularization and the Religion of Humanity

Religion once looked destined to fade into irrelevance as modernity consolidates its hold on human life. The upsurge of religiosity since the late twentieth century, however, suggests another scenario. Secularization theory in the social sciences held that the decline of religion was a corollary of modernization. But many former proponents of this thesis have now abandoned it in the light of mounting evidence to the contrary. "The religious impulse, the quest for meaning that transcends the restricted space of empirical existence in this world," explains the sociologist Peter Berger, "has been a perennial feature of humanity." It is an impulse which it "would require something close to a mutation of the species to extinguish". As for the chances of such a mutation, Berger comments:

> So far it has not happened, and as I have argued, it is unlikely to happen in the foreseeable future. The critique of secularity common to all the resurgent movements is that human existence bereft of transcendence is an impoverished and finally untenable condition.[92]

---

[91] Nehru 2010: 371.

[92] Berger 1999: 13.

The prospects do not look good for ideologies that hope to rid the world of religion. But cosmopolitan humanism has a latent religious dimension of its own. In the struggle with reactionary forces, it might be to its advantage to acknowledge the potential spiritual significance of Enlightenment ideals themselves.

The "religion of humanity" was elaborated as a systematic social doctrine by the nineteenth-century French positivist philosopher Auguste Comte. The phrase is also associated with other thinkers, whether influenced by Comte or not. Sri Aurobindo took it in the broadest sense. He traced its conceptual origins to the eighteenth-century search for a rational alternative to ecclesiastical Christianity and the feudal order it represented. It was then, according to him, that the aim of the religion of humanity was revealed "by a sort of primal intuition; that aim was and it is still to re-create human society in the image of three kindred ideas, liberty, equality and fraternity". Positivism later tried "to formulate the dogmas of this religion, but on too heavily and severely rationalistic a basis for acceptance even by an Age of Reason".[93]

Despite the failure of the religion of humanity in its positivist incarnation, Comte's system and its less ambitious variants were indicators of the Zeitgeist and signposts pointing toward future developments. As the cultural critic Andrew Wernick observes,

> The divinisation of humankind, whether explicit or not, goes to the heart of progressive, post-theistic attempts to rethink modernity's ideological situation.[94]

Wernick lists continuities between the old god and the new one (humanity itself) in substantive characteristics as well as in its psycho-social function:

---

93 Aurobindo 1998b: 294, 298.

94 Wernick 2005: 188.

> "Humanity" inspired and incarnated the highest form of selfless love. It was the ultimate source of moral authority. . . . It was also a "jealous god" and would brook "no other masters among its servants".[95]

Sri Aurobindo singles out some of the same features of this secular religion. Worshipping humanity as its godhead, it has made "the respect, the service, the progress of the human being and human life . . . the chief duty and the chief aim of the human spirit". It rejects any "idol" whose demands are inconsistent with the service of humanity:

> No injunctions of old creeds, religious, political, social or cultural, are valid when they go against its claims.[96]

The religion of humanity, Sri Aurobindo notes, has been "a conscious creed" only for a few. Yet its largely unrecognized influence has stimulated important trends and had pervasive effects on modern societies:

> Humanitarianism has been its most prominent emotional result. Philanthropy, social service and other kindred activities have been its outward expression of good works. Democracy, socialism, pacificism are to a great extent its by-products or at least owe much of their vigour to its inner presence.[97]

Secular human rights activists are described by globalization scholar Nayan Chanda as "the newest incarnations of missionaries, in the broadest sense of the term". Missionaries, he points out, have always been unwitting "agents of globalization". Their secular counterparts now "travel the world not to preach religious sermons but to unite the world around one agenda: protecting the life, liberty, and freedoms of all humans". The director of Human Rights Watch's

---

95 Wernick 2005: 206.

96 Aurobindo 1998b: 295.

97 Ibid.: 294-95.

International Justice Program, interviewed by Chanda, does not relish being compared to a missionary; but he admits "that people who become advocates for others have to be motivated by a sense of mission".[98] The vitality of the religion of humanity today could not be better illustrated.

The mission of this secular faith overlaps with social goals long professed by the old religions. Yet in some ways it has been far more effective than they in changing things for the better. The reason for this, Sri Aurobindo explained, is that unlike orthodox religion it has "acted as a constant intellectual and critical solvent, an unsparing assailant of the thing that is and an unflinching champion of the thing to be, faithful always to the future".[99] But something more is needed, he felt, before the religion of humanity will have a chance of prevailing over the most deep-rooted obstacle to real change in human life, namely, our individual and collective egoism. The idea of humanity, he maintained, has been hampered by the fact that it "has been obliged in an intellectual age to mask its true character of a religion and a thing of the soul and the spirit and to appeal to the vital and physical mind of man rather than his inner being". The result has been at most an "intellectual and sentimental religion of humanity". To fulfil its potential, he contended, this would have to be spiritualized.[100]

The outlines of a spiritual religion of humanity emerge from a deeper interpretation of the Enlightenment ideals of freedom, equality and brotherhood. This deeper significance, Sri Aurobindo believed, was inherent in the original conception of these ideals as essentially Christian aspirations whose spiritual character was disguised in the eighteenth-century struggle against a Church which had become a travesty of Christianity.

---

98 Chanda 2007: 107, 142.

99 Aurobindo 1998b: 296.

100 Ibid.: 297-99.

His reinterpretation of the mantra of the French revolution – his "Asiatic reading of democracy"[101] – seems to owe less to Christian sources, however, than to Vedantic Hinduism:

> When the soul claims freedom, it is the freedom of its self-development, the self-development of the divine in man in all his being. When it claims equality, what it is claiming is that freedom equally for all and the recognition of the same soul, the same godhead in all human beings. When it strives for brotherhood, it is founding that equal freedom of self-development on a common aim, a common life, a unity of mind and feeling founded upon the recognition of this inner spiritual unity. These three things are in fact the nature of the soul; for freedom, equality, unity are the eternal attributes of the Spirit.[102]

The Light of Liberty

Freedom occupies a central place in this vision of a spiritual religion of humanity. Equality and brotherhood (or, better, unity) are extensions or conditions of freedom. "Freedom of self-development" is understood as a spiritual value with socio-political consequences. The relationship of this idea to Western political thought can best be examined with reference to the distinction between negative and positive liberty made by the British political philosopher Isaiah Berlin.

Negative liberty, as Berlin defines it, is "not being interfered with by others". It is freedom from external compulsion, subject to a minimum of socially unavoidable limits. In the spirit of liberalism, Berlin heartily endorses this concept of freedom. Positive liberty, on the other hand, is the freedom of self-mastery or "rational self-direction". It is not *freedom from* restrictions imposed by others, but *freedom to* be fully ourselves. This includes "the traditional self-emancipation

---

101 Aurobindo 2002: 930-32.

102 Aurobindo 1998b: 298, 300.

of ascetics and quietists, of stoics or Buddhist sages". Collectively, it is "at the heart of the demands for national or social self-direction which animate the most powerful and morally just public movements of our time".[103]

As these examples suggest, Berlin by no means denies the value of positive liberty. Its pursuit has played an indispensable and salutary role in human life and he does not try to minimize it. But he warns against its paradoxical tendency to metamorphose into its opposite, despotism:

> The reason within me, if it is to triumph, must eliminate and suppress my 'lower' instincts, my passions and desires, which render me a slave; similarly (the fatal transition from individual to social concepts is almost imperceptible) the higher elements in society . . . may exercise compulsion to rationalise the irrational section of society.[104]

The "sleight of hand" by which tyranny is redefined as liberty depends on inflating the "real" self, whose freedom concerns us, into a "super-personal entity" such as the state. This is then the entity "which, by imposing its collective, or 'organic', single will upon its recalcitrant 'members', achieves its own, and therefore their, 'higher' freedom".[105]

Sri Aurobindo analyzes similarly the contradictions to which the fallacy of the "rational collectivist idea of society" can lead. The justification of totalitarianism in the name of liberty begins with the claim that "the right of the individual to any kind of egoistic freedom as against the State which represents the mind, the will, the good and interest of the whole community . . . is a dangerous fiction." The individual's "infrarational" nature, the argument continues, has to be "thoroughly controlled . . . if he is to become a reasonable being". This can surely be done best

---

103 Berlin 2005: 170, 191, 182, 214.

104 Ibid.: 196.

105 Ibid.: 181, 179.

"by the collective reason and will of the State which is larger, better, more enlightened than the individual's". Thus the individual, "in a happy obedience" to a reason and will superior to his own, will find himself blessed by "a more real freedom than any now claimed by his little separate ego". The relentless logic of this vision of "true" freedom reached its apotheosis, Sri Aurobindo wryly remarks, in "the drilled felicities of Fascist Italy and Nazi Germany".[106]

This is the pathology of what Berlin calls positive liberty. He admits that the concept of negative freedom could likewise be misused – though as a matter of historical fact, he maintains, it has been much less susceptible to manipulation.[107] But in that case, the root of the problem would seem to lie in collectivism rather than in the dangers of a particular understanding of liberty as such. So long as the negative liberty of the individual is adequately safeguarded, as it is to some degree in all liberal democracies, there is no good reason to deny the equal importance of positive liberty.

In modern Indian thought, a distinction akin to Isaiah Berlin's contrast between negative and positive liberty was made before Sri Aurobindo by Swami Vivekananda. Political and spiritual liberty, Vivekananda observed, preoccupied the peoples of ancient Greece and India, respectively. According to him, these two types of liberty are not in conflict. They are essential and complementary values which need to be combined and balanced:

> The Greek sought political liberty. The Hindu has always sought spiritual liberty. Both are one-sided. . . . To care only for spiritual liberty and not for social liberty is a defect, but the opposite is a still greater defect. Liberty of both soul and body is to be striven for.[108]

[106] Aurobindo 1998a: 208-09.

[107] Berlin 2005: 181.

[108] Vivekananda 1989, vol. 6: 86.

This comparison between the types of liberty pursued by the Greeks and the Hindus could be rephrased in terms of negative and positive liberty. Most modern champions of negative liberty appear to be carrying forward the tradition of political theorizing initiated in Periclean Athens. Spiritual liberty, on the other hand, undoubtedly comes under the heading of positive liberty, associated in Berlin's definition with ascetics and Buddhist sages, among others. But the correspondence between these pairs of terms – negative vs. positive and political vs. spiritual – is not exact. Berlin speaks of positive liberty in connection with national liberation movements as well as with individual self-realization. Spiritual liberty, while it involves self-discipline, also normally requires freedom from outside interference. Vivekananda emphasizes this point:

> India has always had this magnificent idea of religious freedom, and you must remember that freedom is the first condition of growth. What you do not make free, will never grow. The idea that you can make others grow and help their growth, that you can direct and guide them, always retaining for yourself the freedom of the teacher, is nonsense, a dangerous lie which has retarded the growth of millions and millions of human beings in this world. Let men have the light of liberty. That is the only condition of growth.[109]

The "lie" Vivekananda condemns corresponds to the "evil" on which Berlin quotes J.S. Mill:

> All errors which [a man] is likely to commit against advice and warning, are far outweighed by the evil of allowing others to constrain him to what they deem his good.[110]

But Vivekananda's reasons for advocating individual freedom, whether in religious or social contexts, were not the same as Mill's and Berlin's. His position was closer to Sri Aurobindo's plea for freedom on ultimately spiritual grounds:

---

109 Vivekananda 1989, vol. 2: 115.

110 Berlin 2005: 174.

> The desires and free seekings of the individual, however egoistic, . . . have behind them a force that . . . needs to be enlightened and trained but must not be suppressed or harnessed exclusively to society's heavy cartwheels . . . ; the stifling of the individual may well be the stifling of the god in man.[111]

Freedom and the Revitalization of India

Keeping in mind these conceptions of freedom found in Western and Indian political and spiritual philosophies, let us return to the person who, during most of the first two decades after Independence, so powerfully shaped the democratic institutions of the free nation known under his leadership as "Nehru's India". Jawaharlal Nehru was passionately committed to the religion of humanity, perhaps mainly in what Sri Aurobindo calls its "intellectual and sentimental" form, but with at least a touch of its deeper spirit. Scattered through Nehru's *Discovery of India* we find hints of a spiritual dimension to both his nationalism and his humanism.

"The Vedanta ideal," Nehru wrote in a passage on Swami Vivekananda, "was of the solidarity of man and his inborn divine nature; to see God in man is the real God-vision." While this may not have been exactly Nehru's own vision, he spoke approvingly of Vedanta as "not only spiritual but rational and in harmony with scientific investigations of external nature". He appreciated Vivekananda's "stress on the necessity for liberty and equality and the raising of the masses".[112] The "liberty of both soul and body" insisted on by Vivekananda was what Nehru wanted for the Indian people. It is true that the body came first for him, before there could be any question of higher preoccupations. But Vivekananda sometimes expressed the same sentiment, as when he burst out on one occasion:

---

111 Aurobindo 2005b: 196.

112 Nehru 2010: 369.

> Bread! Bread! I do not believe in a God, who cannot give me bread here, giving me eternal bliss in heaven! Pooh! India is to be raised, the poor are to be fed, education is to be spread. . . . More bread, more opportunity for everybody![113]

In an address to the Constituent Assembly on 22 January 1947, Nehru described the Assembly's "first task". It was

> to free India through a new constitution, to feed the starving people, and to clothe the naked masses, and to give every Indian the fullest opportunity to develop himself according to his capacity.[114]

Obviously, the freeing of India in the sense of ending foreign rule was not up to the Constituent Assembly. But the Indian freedom struggle, like other such movements, was not only about negative liberty for the country and its citizens. Even Berlin, with all his reservations about positive liberty, acknowledges that "to offer political rights, or safeguards against intervention by the State, to men who are half-naked, illiterate, underfed and diseased is to mock their condition".[115] Nehru wanted the constitution to guarantee, as far as possible, what Sri Aurobindo calls "freedom of self-development" to all Indians. In *The Discovery of India*, Nehru had written:

> I was not interested in making some political arrangement which would enable our people to carry on more or less as before, only a little better. I felt they had vast stores of suppressed energy and ability, and I wanted to release these and make them feel young and vital again. India, constituted as she is, cannot play a secondary part in the world. She will either count for a great deal or not count at all.[116]

---

113 Vivekananda 1989, vol. 4: 368.

114 Corbridge and Harriss 2000: 20.

115 Berlin 2005: 171.

116 Nehru 2010: 48.

National liberation had psychological and even spiritual aspects for Nehru in addition to its political and economic sides. Speaking of his and other nationalist leaders' efforts "to revitalize India", he wrote:

> We aimed high and looked far. Probably we were often foolish, from the point of view of opportunist politics, but at no time did we forget that our main purpose was to raise the whole level of the Indian people, psychologically and spiritually and also, of course, politically and economically. It was the building up of that real inner strength of the people that we were after, knowing that the rest would inevitably follow. We had to wipe out some generations of shameful subservience and timid submission to an arrogant alien authority.[117]

The freedom struggle succeeded to a considerable extent in reviving this inner strength and self-respect. Besides Gandhi, the "Father of the Nation", no one did more to bring this about than the man who emerged as the undisputed head of the government of independent India.

For all his accomplishments, it is generally agreed that Nehru failed in one major area which was central to what he hoped to achieve. In order "to feed the starving people", he imposed a combination of socialism and protectionism on the country. This approach had to be abandoned within three decades after his death. In his overreaction to the memory of colonial capitalism, Tharoor notes, Nehru created "a state that ensured political freedom but presided over economic stagnation; that regulated entrepreneurial activity through a system of licenses, permits and quotas that promoted both corruption and inefficiency but did little to promote growth".[118] In the economic sphere, in other words, Nehru

---

117 Nehru 2010: 49.

118 Tharoor 2013: 206-07.

underestimated the need for negative liberty and ignored the consequences of curbing individual initiative. Besides, he seemed to forget his own realization that in modern times "isolation was both undesirable and impossible". His economic policies were at odds with his vision of a future "of intimate co-operation politically, economically, and culturally, between India and the other countries of the world".[119]

Nehru once spoke to the French writer and statesman André Malraux of the difficulty of "creating a secular State in a religious country".[120] But the notion of secularism did not imply for Nehru a complete rejection of religion and spirituality. He recognized the necessity of "some faith . . . in things of the spirit which are beyond the scope of our physical world, some reliance on moral, spiritual, and idealistic conceptions, or else we have no anchorage, no objectives or purpose in life." This passage in *The Discovery of India* continues:

> It is therefore with the temper and approach of science, allied to philosophy, and with reverence for all that lies beyond, that we must face life. Thus we may develop an integral vision of life which embraces in its wide scope the past and the present, with all their heights and depths, and look with serenity towards the future.[121]

Such integrality, Nehru felt, should come easily to Indians. Anything less would be unworthy of the culture they inherit. This culture is that of an ancient civilization, stable at its core, yet assimilative and always changing. Its historical development has prepared it well to respond to the stimulating conditions of the modern, globalized world. As Nehru put it:

> The essential basis of Indian thought for ages past . . . fits in with the scientific temper and approach, as well as with

119 Nehru 2010: 41.

120 Guha 2007: 233.

121 Nehru 2010: 571-72.

> internationalism. It is based on a fearless search for truth, on the solidarity of man, even on the divinity of everything living, and on the free and cooperative development of the individual and the species, ever to greater freedom and higher stages of human growth.[122]

When Jawaharlal Nehru passed away on 27 May 1964, tributes flooded in from all over the world. One came from Pondicherry. Sri Aurobindo was no more, but the head of his ashram, the Frenchwoman Mirra Alfassa, better known as the Mother, issued a message:

> Nehru leaves his body but his soul is one with the Soul of India that lives for Eternity.[123]

122 Nehru 2010: 573.

123 The Mother 2004: 360.

6

Serenity, Courage and Wisdom

Reinhold Niebuhr, Sri Aurobindo and the American Dream

Some things are up to us and some are not up to us.

– Epictetus, *Encheiridion* 1 in Irvine 2009: 86

For all of us who over-identify the human future with the success of our own temporary projects . . . maintaining that prophetic sense of God's transcendence is . . . crucial to having a realistic view of where you are in the world, but also crucial to sustaining your own motivation to continue to work at it.

– Robin Lovin 2004

Niebuhr Revisited

THE history of religion in the United States, from the colonial era to quite recent times, has been largely the history of its Judeo–Christian traditions. On the other hand, freedom, pluralism and exploration are at the heart of what this country represents. Besides the dominant Protestantism, there are several other strands in American religion which cannot be overlooked if we want to understand its past or glimpse its future. The indigenous religious cultures of the Native Americans share a message of harmony with nature which we ignore at our peril. Nor can we disregard the growing presence of religions from all parts of Asia. In the early nineteenth century, some of the Transcendentalists were among the first Americans to be inspired by Eastern spirituality, as so many have been since. The Parliament of Religions in Chicago in 1893 was the beginning of organized interfaith dialogue and a landmark in the spread of Asian teachings to the West. However, the most dramatic surge in religious diversity has occurred as a result of the influx from the non-Western world since the passage of the Immigration Act of 1965.

As a non-Christian who has spent equal time in the United States and India, I keep all this in mind when I read the works of Reinhold Niebuhr (1892–1971). A Protestant theologian and political philosopher active in the mid-twentieth century, Niebuhr belonged formally to America's religious mainstream. But he was critical of many things in both liberal and conservative American Protestantism, and his insights into the social and political problems of his day were perhaps more influential outside the church than within it. During his lifetime, interreligious dialogue in America did not extend much beyond conversations among Protestants, Catholics and Jews. Now, however, Niebuhr must be reassessed in a more radically pluralistic and multicultural age confronted with issues he could not have anticipated.

By comparing his thought with that of Sri Aurobindo (1872–1950), the foremost spiritual philosopher of modern India, I intend to suggest Niebuhr's continued relevance in a larger framework than that of the Protestant Christianity and American secularism to which he primarily addressed himself. I hope it will also become clear that the writings of Sri Aurobindo, which have only begun to be discovered outside of India, have much to offer in this larger framework.

American Exceptionalism

The founding documents of the United States guaranteed religious freedom. They made possible the eventual emergence of a pluralism such as could hardly have been conceived in the eighteenth century. We now take this for granted. Yet, considering the strength of religious feeling throughout much of the history of the colonies and the early republic, it could easily have been otherwise. It has been argued that it was mainly the timing of the Revolution that saved the United States from becoming an officially Christian nation.[1] Independence was achieved when the new country had leaders who were under the influence of the European Enlightenment. Evangelical Christianity was then in a state of temporary exhaustion between the so-called First Great Awakening of the 1730s and 1740s and the Second Great Awakening which swept through the land in the early decades of the nineteenth century. It may have been partly in reaction to such excesses of religious enthusiasm that some of the founding fathers were drawn to the abstract Deism reflected in the Declaration of Independence. These were the circumstances under which the nation came into being as a distinct political entity.

But adopting a secular constitution could not stop Americans from seeing themselves as a chosen people, a self-image with decidedly biblical overtones. Reinhold Niebuhr discerned "a deep layer of Messianic consciousness in the mind of America".[2] He warned of the danger this poses, now that the country finds itself wielding unprecedented power in the world community. The Puritans had arrived in New England convinced of their God-given mission to create a society free from the vices of Europe. Their doctrine of human depravity was at the opposite pole from the Jeffersonian optimism that prevailed at the time of the Revolution. Yet Niebuhr notes a peculiar affinity between the New England Calvinists and the Virginian Deists in their understanding of our collective

1 Wills 2007: 7: "It is probable that the great break with history signified by Disestablishment could have taken place at no other time in American history than the founding era."

2 Niebuhr 2008: 69.

character and destiny. For all their differences, both of these groups which shaped the national mentality and institutions believed that America had a divinely bestowed mission "to make a new beginning in a corrupt world".[3]

The resulting illusions of unique national virtue and innocence are now commonly known as "American exceptionalism". Though this expression does not occur in *The Irony of American History*, Niebuhr's book contains a critique of the exceptionalist mindset that is as relevant today as when it was published in 1952. "The American dream is not particularly unique," he admits. "Almost every nation has had a version of it." Nor is the dream itself necessarily a bad thing, apart from the collective egoism associated with it. But recent circumstances have made the United States unusually susceptible to temptations of what Niebuhr calls "managing history". Illusions about the ability to do so invariably involve, he observes,

> miscalculations about both the power and the wisdom of the managers and of the weakness and the manageability of the historical 'stuff' which is to be managed.[4]

The underlying problem is that

> modern man lacks the humility to accept the fact that the whole drama of history is enacted in a frame of meaning too large for human comprehension or management. It is a drama in which fragmentary meanings can be discerned within a penumbra of mystery.[5]

Prosperity and Happiness

One of the illusions to which Americans are prone is the belief that our prosperity, whose causes include many fortuitous

[3] Niebuhr 2008: 24-25.

[4] Ibid.: 72.

[5] Ibid.: 88.

factors, is purely the reward of our merit. By this self-flattering assumption, Niebuhr noted, we "have complicated our spiritual problem for the days of adversity which we are bound to experience".[6] Moreover, the chances of such adversity are increased by a bourgeois ideology which overestimates the self-regulating capacity of the market. The glorification of the principles of *laissez-faire*, Niebuhr pointed out, "makes for tardiness in dealing with the instability of a free economy". He added presciently:

> Some believe that the lessons taught in the great depression of 1929 have been so well learned that a recurrence of such a catastrophe is impossible; but it is not altogether certain that this is true. . . . From the viewpoint of Europe, whose economic health has become so dependent on the American giant that a tremor in our system creates serious shocks in the world economy, we remain an irritatingly incalculable element in world stability.[7]

Due to the resources and opportunities offered by a huge continent, America has long been able to alleviate social tensions and reduce internal dissent by resorting to the safety valve of territorial, economic and technological expansion. Unfortunately, as Niebuhr warned over half a century ago, "this expansion cannot go on forever".[8] Thus America cannot avoid facing in an acute form the crisis of Western modernity, whose centuries-long expansionist thrust has been halted by the finiteness of the globe.

The problem with modernity lies not in the idea of progress itself, but in the fixation on its externals and the neglect of its inner dimension. That misplaced emphasis has led to a dangerously unhealthy imbalance. At this point, the religious resources of the American tradition might have been expected

6 Niebuhr 2008: 49.

7 Ibid.: 105.

8 Ibid.: 29.

to come to our rescue. Religion, if anything, should be able to serve as a corrective to the greed and materialism of an unsustainable way of life – the so-called American way of life, which a recent US president declared to be non-negotiable.[9] The difficulty, however, is that religion was complicit almost from the beginning in the materialism that has become virtually synonymous with America in the eyes of its critics.

Niebuhr explains how the austere Puritans gradually became infatuated with worldly comforts and luxuries. Once they had survived the initial ordeals of life in the wilderness, the settlers found the natural abundance of this fertile continent conducive to a more plentiful existence than they had ever imagined. In the course of time, gratitude for God's blessings gave way to a more self-congratulatory attitude. This was partly due to the doctrine of "special providence", the belief that particular acts of divine intervention reward virtue and punish vice. If so, clearly God was pleased with the Puritans and they had good reason to be pleased with themselves. This, in Niebuhr's view, was one of "two elements in the Calvinist creed, which transmuted it from a faith which would take prosperity and adversity in its stride to a religion which became preoccupied with the prosperity of the new community". The related Calvinist belief that "godliness is profitable to all things"[10] contributed to the same attitude.

For the American Puritans, therefore, virtue was the source of prosperity. The Jeffersonians, on the other hand, expected prosperity to lead to the flowering of the social virtues. Starting from the anti-Calvinist conviction of the innate goodness of human nature, they reasoned that if everyone had ample means

---

9 George H.W. Bush, press conference at Earth Summit, Rio de Janeiro, as reported in *The Guardian* on 1 June 1992 (Aall and Hille 2010: 98).

10 Niebuhr 2008: 49-50.

to satisfy their legitimate needs and desires, the motives for crime, exploitation and conflict would disappear. Regrettably, Niebuhr remarks, this excellent theory overlooks "the perennial conflicts of power and pride which may arise on every level of 'abundance' since human desires grow with the means of their gratification".[11] In any case, whether virtue was thought to be the basis of prosperity or prosperity the basis of virtue, their close association in the otherwise contradictory Puritan and Jeffersonian currents of American culture fostered moral confusion. The outcome of it all, Niebuhr maintained, was "a preoccupation with the material circumstances of life which expressed a more consistent bourgeois ethos than that of even the most advanced nations of Europe".[12]

With his lifelong passion for democracy and social justice, Reinhold Niebuhr was certainly not unsympathetic to the spirit of Thomas Jefferson's great proclamation in the preamble to the Declaration of Independence:

> We hold these truths to be self-evident, that all men are created equal, that they are endowed by their Creator with certain unalienable Rights, that among these are Life, Liberty and the pursuit of Happiness.

Nevertheless, Niebuhr voiced concern about the place that the pursuit of happiness, as commonly understood, has come to occupy in American conceptions of the aim of life. "Happiness" has a broad range of meanings. Jefferson's own idea of personal happiness was far from hedonistic, influenced as it was by Epicurus's identification of happiness with a tranquility achieved through self-discipline. But for most members of an increasingly materialistic society, "happiness" depended on external conditions. The Industrial Revolution linked happiness to the growing ease and luxury produced

---

11 Niebuhr 2008: 30.

12 Ibid.: 53.

by the continual advance of technology. As heirs to this legacy, modern Americans are exceptionally ill-equipped to deal with a decline in their accustomed level of opulence. Yet sooner or later, setbacks are inevitable in a situation where, as Niebuhr observed, "the paradise of our domestic security is suspended in a hell of global insecurity".[13] He wrote:

> The real question is whether a religion or a culture is capable of interpreting life in a dimension sufficiently profound . . . to achieve a serenity . . . which is something less but also something more than "happiness."[14]

This is a question that a nation shopping for happiness in a world of vanishing resources, environmental crises and international instability might do well to start asking itself.

The Serenity Prayer

Reinhold Niebuhr not only diagnosed America's addiction to a delusive happiness resting on crumbling foundations; he also provided a practical aid to the attainment of an inner serenity less vulnerable to the vicissitudes of history. He offered this remedy almost inadvertently, yet a remarkable number of people have found it effective. It takes the form of a mantra known as the "Serenity Prayer". These are Niebuhr's most famous words:

> God, give us grace to accept with serenity the things that cannot be changed, courage to change the things that should be changed, and the wisdom to distinguish the one from the other.[15]

The immense popularity of the Serenity Prayer has brought it well-deserved attention, but sometimes in ways that obscure its relation to the subtleties of Niebuhr's thought. The

---

13 Niebuhr 2008: 7.

14 Ibid.: 54.

15 Sifton 2005: 7.

theologian's celebrated prayer has a simplicity that can be deceptive, especially when his concise sentence is further shortened to the version that was adopted by Alcoholics Anonymous and is in general circulation:

> God, grant me the serenity to accept the things I cannot change, courage to change the things I can, and wisdom to know the difference.[16]

Niebuhr's daughter, Elisabeth Sifton, tells us that her father's friends "were amused by the irony of having the austere Niebuhr associated with feel-good Hallmark sentimentalities". She remarks:

> All too often the Serenity Prayer has been construed as a way to say something clever about life's difficulties, rather than as a true petition for grace and wisdom in an impossible world.

She acknowledges that Niebuhr "was happy to have his prayers used in whatever context people wanted or needed them, and he respected the intense gratitude that AA members expressed for the Serenity Prayer".[17] At the same time, the fact that toward the end of the Second World War the prayer was printed on cards given to soldiers going into battle reflects an aspect of its original spirit that tends to be forgotten in its current association with the "twelve-step programs" of the self-help culture.

In any case this sentence is quintessential Niebuhr, though it has often been cited without attribution or erroneously ascribed to a variety of other sources. In fact, there is no serious rival candidate for its authorship. No convincing reasons have been given for doubting that it is Niebuhr's. However, there

---

[16] This is the version that is almost always reproduced, with minor variations, when the prayer is printed in a calligraphic form or illustrated with photography or artwork.

[17] Sifton 2005: 294, 342, 346.

is some confusion about when it was written. Sifton traced it to 1943 in her memoir, *The Serenity Prayer: Faith and Politics in Times of Peace and War*. But recent research pushes its date of origin back to the early or mid-1930s, since variants of it – evidently due to oral transmission – began to appear in print by 1936. An essay published by Niebuhr in 1934, "The Assurance of Grace",[18] shows that he was preoccupied around that time with precisely the ideas that are packed so succinctly into the Serenity Prayer.

No doubt, writing this brief prayer was a minor incident in the eventful period of Niebuhr's life to which it seems to belong. He could not have foreseen then how it would take on a life of its own. So when he was questioned about it years later, it is not surprising that he was unable to pinpoint when he had composed it. His typically modest and candid answer was that it "may have been spooking around for years, even centuries, but I don't think so. I honestly do believe that I wrote it myself".[19] No doubt, some of the ideas contained in the Serenity Prayer had indeed been "spooking around" for a long time – at least since the days of the Stoics. However, this only means that its originality lies not in its separate ingredients, but in their unique combination. The resulting formula expresses a distinctive attitude which is nothing if not Niebuhrian.

Throughout his life, Niebuhr stressed "the importance of accommodating the vision of perfection to an imperfect world, without losing the urge to perfect the world".[20] To lose the urge to perfect the world is defeatism. To imagine that the world will easily let itself be perfected is a sentimental illusion. Exaggerating the obstacles to change and underestimating them can be equally fatal to responsible action. In the words

---

18 Niebuhr 1986: 61-71.

19 Shapiro 2008.

20 Niebuhr 1986: 70.

of the prayer, we need the courage to change what can and should be changed. Elsewhere Niebuhr speaks of softening the incongruities of life; we must try to narrow the gap between how things should be and how they actually are. But there will be things we cannot change, for "all such strategies cannot finally overcome the fragmentary character of human existence. The final wisdom of life requires, not the annulment of incongruity but the achievement of serenity within and above it." Niebuhr goes on to suggest the need for a larger outlook than the normal perspective of our rational and egoistic consciousness:

> Nothing that is worth doing can be achieved in our lifetime; therefore we must be saved by hope. Nothing which is true or beautiful or good makes complete sense in any immediate context of history; therefore we must be saved by faith. Nothing we do, however virtuous, can be accomplished alone; therefore we are saved by love. No virtuous act is quite as virtuous from the standpoint of our friend or foe as it is from our standpoint. Therefore we must be saved by the final form of love which is forgiveness.[21]

Reinhold Niebuhr and Sri Aurobindo

Niebuhr's thought surprisingly resembles at some points that of an older contemporary of his in India. Sri Aurobindo formulated his philosophy against a very different cultural background, but like Niebuhr he applied the insights of an ancient spiritual tradition to the problems of the modern world. This seems to be the explanation of similarities in their thinking, since there is no reason to believe that either had any significant knowledge of the other's writings.

Niebuhr had an ambivalent attitude toward Indian mysticism. He was not entirely hostile to it in the spirit of religious exclusivism that even today is all too common among

21 Niebuhr 2008: 62-63.

Christians. In a passage in his first major work, *Moral Man and Immoral Society*, he quotes the nineteenth-century Hindu saint Sri Ramakrishna as saying:

> I have come to the stage of realisation in which I see that God is walking in every human form and manifesting himself alike in the sage and in the sinner.

Between references to Jesus, St. Francis and Paul, Niebuhr cites Ramakrishna's words to illustrate

> the capacity of the religious imagination to view the immediate and the imperfect from the perspective of the absolute and the transcendent.[22]

Often, though, he speaks less favorably of the religions and societies of India and of Asia in general. He writes, for example:

> Spiritually the Orient is informed by religions which are either mystic and pantheistic such as Buddhism and Hinduism; or humanistic and collectivist such as the Confucianism of China or the Shintoism of Japan. Pantheistic religions can find no significance for the individual in the integral unity of his spiritual and physical life. The purpose of religious redemption is the annulment of individual existence and its incorporation into a divine unity.

After contrasting this with Confucianism – which, despite its humanistic character, also allegedly fails to grant the individual a "significant place in the scheme of things" – Niebuhr concludes:

> There is thus no spiritual basis in the Orient for what we know as the "dignity of the individual".[23]

Such depreciations might be taken as signs of Eurochauvinism, except that it is not only Asian culture which Niebuhr faults for

---

22 Niebuhr 2005: 39.

23 Niebuhr 2008: 124-25.

inadequately supporting individuality. For the same reason he criticizes even the classical Western world-view, in contrast to the biblical tradition. Even today, he asserts, the concept of individuality "belongs to that class of certainties of modern man about himself which his own history has gradually dissipated".[24]

But as regards the Orient and particularly the social impact of the mystical religions of India, the notion that these religions provide no spiritual basis for the dignity of the individual is not fully consistent even with Niebuhr's own statements. In *The Nature and Destiny of Man*, he points out that all mystic religions "have the characteristic of accentuating individuality inasfar as individuality is inherent in the capacity for self-consciousness emphasized in mysticism and is something more than mere bodily particularity". On the other hand, he goes on to assert that "all mystic philosophies ultimately lose the very individuality which they first emphasize, because they sink finite particularity in a distinctionless divine ground of existence".[25] But the admitted accentuation of individuality by these philosophies, in all but the most advanced and uncommon stages of spiritual realization, surely cannot be discounted in considering their implications for the value of individual existence. India's "spiritual individualism", as Swami Vivekananda called it,[26] has always counterbalanced the social tendency, common to all ancient cultures, to subordinate the individual to the demands of the collectivity.

---

24 Niebuhr 1996, vol. 1: 21. Sri Aurobindo similarly observes the modern paradox that the "discovery by individual free-thought of universal laws of which the individual is almost a by-product and by which he must necessarily be governed . . . seems to lead logically to the suppression of that very individual freedom which made the discovery and the attempt at all possible." (Aurobindo 1998a: 21.)

25 Niebuhr 1996: 15.

26 Vivekananda 1989, vol. 8: 269.

In any case, it is not true that all mysticism in the East or the West culminates in the self-annihilation of the individual in the absolute. The view of Sri Aurobindo, one of the great mystics of recent times, is that "the right relation of the soul with the Supreme" is "neither to assert egoistically its separate being nor to blot itself out in the Indefinable".[27] This broadly agrees with the Judeo–Christian position championed by Niebuhr. Nor is it an unusual view within the Indian tradition.

But even if this were not so, what matters today is not what a tradition may have said in the past, but how the heirs of that tradition are reshaping it under present conditions. Sri Aurobindo was one of India's leading thinkers in the twentieth century. It is significant, therefore, that he considered the "deeper truth which individualism has discovered" to be of the utmost importance. The individual, he wrote,

> demands freedom, space, initiative for his soul, for his nature, for that puissant and tremendous thing which society so much distrusts and has laboured in the past either to suppress altogether or to relegate to the purely spiritual field, an individual thought, will and conscience.

He added:

> That is an idea, a truth which, intellectually recognised and given its full exterior and superficial significance by Europe, agrees at its root with the profoundest and highest spiritual conceptions of Asia and has a large part to play in the moulding of the future.[28]

Reinhold Niebuhr's comments on Eastern religions and what he calls "the sleeping cultures of the Orient"[29] are based on second-hand stereotypes. In contrast to his masterly analysis of the phases of Western civilization, he accepts misleading

27 Aurobindo 1999: 22.

28 Aurobindo 1998a: 24-25.

29 Niebuhr 2008: 123.

Orientalist generalizations and largely overlooks the creative responses of contemporary Asia to modernity. But we need not be detained by his misconceptions about things with which he had only a passing acquaintance. If we look closely at the message distilled in the Serenity Prayer, we find that the Protestant theologian has more in common with the Indian philosopher than we might have expected.

God, Us and Things

The Serenity Prayer is concerned with the relations among three entities: God, us and things: "*God*, give *us* grace to accept with serenity the *things* that cannot be changed. . . ." These sum up all that we can imagine or experience as reality in its transcendent, individual and universal aspects. In Niebuhr's prayer, the transcendent (God) is addressed in the second person; the individual perspective is represented by ourselves, speaking in the first person (us) as separate conscious beings; what remains is the universal, referred to in the third person by the all-inclusive designation "things". These three dimensions of existence also correspond roughly to three levels of consciousness. God is suprarational; we are at least partly rational; outside things, as well as the most problematic part of human nature in oneself and in others, are largely infrarational. Niebuhr and Sri Aurobindo both distinguish the suprarational, the rational and the infrarational using the same terms or similar ones, such as "ultrarational" in Niebuhr's case and "supramental" in Sri Aurobindo's. Their points of agreement are due to a great extent to their shared recognition of the interaction of these three domains in the infinitely complex phenomenon we call life.

The Serenity Prayer supposes a tension between "us" and two types of "things" – those we can change and those we cannot. "God" is invoked to help us resolve this tension. But God is not part of our normal human experience and we may rationally doubt the existence of any such entity. In that case, we could modify the opening of the sentence to express a more self-reliant attitude: "*May we accept* with serenity the things that cannot be changed. . . ." Without God and grace it is no longer a prayer, but otherwise the original idea seems to be intact.

Minus the grace of God, the formula is reminiscent of Stoicism. The ancient Stoic discipline distinguishes what is under our control from what is not. It teaches us to calm our minds by training ourselves not to worry about things that "are not up to us", as Epictetus puts it at the beginning of his *Handbook*. This frees us from being troubled by external circumstances. We no longer react to the behavior of people or the turns of events with anger, grief or other negative emotions. Much of the benefit that so many derive from the Serenity Prayer may be due to the dose of Stoic philosophy they receive from it.

Niebuhr appreciated the nobility of Stoicism and its refusal "to lobby in the courts of the Almighty for special favors", as William James criticized Christianity for doing. He considered the Stoic outlook to be true "as far as it goes",[30] but thought it did not go far enough. The Stoics developed effective methods of strengthening the rational element in human nature against our irrational tendencies. However, humanity seems to have a deeply ingrained intuition of something which reason cannot fathom, but which is not merely irrational. Summarizing the relationship of the human being to God and the world as the Jewish and Christian traditions see it, Niebuhr states:

> It is not assumed that God's purposes can be fully measured by any measuring rod of human ideals. In one of the greatest books of religious poetry, the book of Job, man questions the justice of God in terms of human standards, but is finally

[30] Niebuhr 1986: 37.

> overwhelmed by the majesty and mystery of existence.... Something of that idea, i.e., that the world is intensely meaningful, even though its meaning transcends human comprehension, runs as one strain through all profound religion. . . . It expresses a trust in life even when the immediate facts of life seem to outrage our conception of what life ought to be: "Though he slay me yet will I trust him" (Job 13:15).[31]

As if to confirm that this is indeed a strain that runs through profound religion everywhere, Sri Aurobindo writes similarly in his *Essays on the Gita*, even alluding to the same biblical verse:

> If we accept at all, as the Gita accepts, the existence of God, that is to say of the omnipresent, omniscient, omnipotent, yet always transcendent Being who manifests the world and Himself in the world, . . . then the human being has to start from a great, a difficult act of faith. Finding himself in a world which is apparently a chaos of battling powers, a clash of vast and obscure forces, a life which subsists only by constant change and death, menaced from every side by pain, suffering, evil and destruction, he has to see the omnipresent Deity in it all and conscious that of this enigma there must be a solution and beyond this Ignorance in which he dwells a Knowledge that reconciles, he has to take his stand upon this faith, "Though Thou slay me, yet will I trust in Thee."[32]

Serenity, Courage and Wisdom

The supplication for the grace of God in the Serenity Prayer is not, then, an empty formality. Serenity was intimately associated with grace in Niebuhr's experience. Those "who live with any degree of serenity", he wrote, "live by some assurance of grace". He added:

---

31 Niebuhr 1986: 14.

32 Aurobindo 1997b: 47-48.

> In every life there must at least be times and seasons when the good is felt as a present possession and not as a far-off goal.[33]

The experience of grace that intervenes at these times can be interpreted as "the apprehension of the absolute from the perspective of the relative. The unachieved is in some sense felt to be achieved or realized."[34] It is a sign of the mysterious workings of the power shaping our lives that adverse circumstances are often most favorable for tasting "the peace of God, which passeth all understanding".[35] This is not a mere consolation prize for those who are defeated by life. It is "the good" itself, the goal of our existence, momentarily "felt as a present possession".

But the serenity that temporarily reconciles us to the world as it is could easily undermine our commitment to making the world more like it should be. Therefore Niebuhr prayed simultaneously for serenity and courage. The kind of courage he had in mind, like his serenity, was rooted in a deeply religious consciousness. He explained that

> there must always be a religious element in the hope of a just society. Without the ultrarational hopes and passions of religion no society will ever have the courage to conquer despair and attempt the impossible; for the vision of a just society is an impossible one, which can be approximated only by those who do not regard it as impossible.

In the same paradoxical vein, he continued:

> The truest visions of religion are illusions, which may be partially realised by being resolutely believed. For what religion believes to be true is not wholly true but ought to be true; and may become true if its truth is not doubted.[36]

---

33 Niebuhr 1986: 64.

34 Ibid.: 62.

35 Philippians 4.7.

36 Niebuhr 2005: 53.

In the Serenity Prayer, Niebuhr expressed his sense of the need to balance ethical striving and the courage to work for change, on the one hand, with a relaxation of moral tension and acquiescence in the world's unavoidable imperfections, on the other. This acquiescence is inwardly liberating, though it may seem an admission of defeat in the struggle to realize our vision. The key to resolving potential contradictions between serenity and courage lies in the third and rarest quality asked for in the prayer: wisdom. In so far as it is within human reach, Niebuhr ascribes wisdom, too, to grace:

> Thus wisdom about our destiny is dependent upon a humble recognition of the limits of our knowledge and our power. Our most reliable understanding is the fruit of "grace" in which faith completes our ignorance without pretending to possess its certainties as knowledge.[37]

The Serenity Prayer and Integral Yoga

The dialectical interplay of opposites that pervades Niebuhr's thinking is equally characteristic of Sri Aurobindo's. Affirmation and negation are one of these pairs of opposites. Abstract in appearance, their relationship has considerable practical consequences. According to Sri Aurobindo,

> it is the right way of self-affirmation and self-negation taken together in place of the wrong, because ignorant, way of the ego . . . that we have to discover.[38]

This discovery could be said to underlie his method of spiritual practice. As we will see, there is a structural correspondence between the three sections of the Serenity Prayer and the outline of a central part of Sri Aurobindo's Integral Yoga. Niebuhr's prayer shows that he was also seeking to combine self-affirmation and self-negation. Serenity requires self-abnegation;

---

37 Niebuhr 1996, vol. 2: 321.

38 Aurobindo 2005a: 649.

courage shows a mood of self-affirmation; only wisdom can discover how to harmonize these seeming contraries.

It "is common ground to all thinking humanity," Sri Aurobindo noted, to suppose that the human being "is capable of self-development and of some approach at least to an ideal standard of perfection which his mind is able to conceive, fix before it and pursue."[39] Only a minority may be seriously preoccupied with this and there are differences of opinion about how far human nature is perfectible even at best. But the sharpest disagreements are over what is meant by "perfection". Various ideals, differing in the relative importance they give to the inner and the outer life, have been proposed in Eastern and Western civilizations from ancient to modern times. At one extreme is the quietism of the ascetic religious ideal which takes the world to be irredeemable and seeks salvation in the serenity of the spirit. At the other extreme is the activism of the mundane ideal of a rational society to be achieved through gradual progress or a revolutionary upheaval.

Some have attempted to balance the religious and mundane ideals, quietism and activism, serene acceptance and courageous struggle, the pull of self-negation and the push of self-affirmation. Today more than ever before, an adequate response to the challenges and complexities of existence would seem to require such a harmonization of apparent contraries. For Sri Aurobindo the ideal worth pursuing was an integral perfection, at once spiritual and this-worldly, individual and collective. His Yoga of self-perfection aspires toward this ideal. It begins with individual transformation.

The first step is to cultivate equanimity, or equality as the Sanskrit term used in the *Bhagavad-Gītā* can be translated. The practitioner must become capable of "an even acceptance of

39 Aurobindo 2005b: 616.

all God's workings within and around him".[40] This has several stages described in detail in *The Synthesis of Yoga*. Like Niebuhr's serenity which is a gift of grace, Sri Aurobindo's equality may be achieved to some extent by personal effort, but is complete only when our being is filled with "the eternal tranquillity of the Infinite".[41]

The second part of the Yoga of self-perfection is concerned with developing all the sides of our personality and heightening all our capacities for thought, feeling and action. This cannot be done without "a searching and subtle self-knowledge" and "a vigilant and insistent will of self-modification and self-transformation".[42] While a number of dynamic qualities are needed, one that is representative of them all is courage. If the discipline of self-perfection is to be a preparation for world-changing action, unshakable courage is essential. Sri Aurobindo distinguished two forms of it. "Passive courage" or fearlessness must be complemented by an "active courage" consisting of "the daring to undertake any enterprise however difficult or apparently impossible and carry it through in spite of all dangers, suffering, failures, obstacles and oppositions".[43] One is reminded of Niebuhr's ultrarationally inspired "courage to conquer despair and attempt the impossible".

The juxtaposition of these first two divisions of the Yoga, with their contrasting emphases on passivity and activity, translates into psychological practice the philosophical intention of reconciling self-negation and self-affirmation. But their successful combination depends on access to the wisdom that "unifies, marries contrasts in a single harmony". This is

---

40 Aurobindo 2005b: 722

41 Ibid.: 692.

42 Ibid.: 739.

43 Aurobindo 2001b: 1469.

sought in the third part of the discipline of self-perfection. The key to the entire endeavor is the transition from a life precariously guided by reason, the faculty that "divides, fixes details and contrasts them",[44] to a life illumined by a deeper wisdom that unites and harmonizes. Yet the ability to distinguish things is not lost, but enhanced by the flowering of the faculties of a suprarational consciousness.

What most distinguishes the mystic from the theologian is his assurance that these exceptional faculties are fully attainable. But there is little point in speaking of them as long as our reasoning mind itself is subject to infrarational influences that distort its workings and vitiate its conclusions. The principal factor usually responsible for the mixture of reason and unreason in our thinking is the intrusion of the ego.

Pessimism, Optimism and the American Dream

The problem of the ego preoccupied both of our thinkers. Within the frameworks of their respective traditions, Sri Aurobindo and Reinhold Niebuhr agree on the nature of the human ego as a false center of existence. Sri Aurobindo puts it philosophically:

> This is the sign of the original ignorance which is the root of the ego, that it can only think with itself as centre as if it were the All. . . . This mental self-sufficiency of man creates a system of false accountantship which prevents us from drawing the right and full value from life. . . . To recognise that we, or rather the results and appearances we call ourselves, are only a partial movement of this infinite Movement and that it is that infinite which we have to know, to be consciously and to fulfil faithfully, is the commencement of true living.[45]

In an essay on Augustine, Niebuhr states from a Christian perspective much the same view of the nature of the ego:

44 Aurobindo 1997a: 424.

45 Aurobindo 2005a: 80.

> Man, according to the biblical view, may use his freedom to make himself falsely the center of existence; but this does not change the fact that love rather than self-love is the law of his existence, in the sense that man can only be healthy, and his communities at peace, if man is drawn out of himself and saved from the self-defeating consequences of self-love.[46]

Niebuhr's misleading reputation as a pessimist is largely due to his keen insight into the role of the ego in human life even at its most virtuous. In *Moral Man and Immoral Society*, he comments:

> In analysing the limits of reason in morality it is important to begin by recognising that the force of egoistic impulse is much more powerful than any but the most astute psychological analysts and the most rigorous devotees of introspection realise. If it is defeated on a lower or more obvious level, it will express itself in more subtle forms. If it is defeated by social impulse it insinuates itself into the social impulse, so that a man's devotion to his community always means the expression of a transferred egoism as well as of altruism.[47]

Sri Aurobindo summarizes the same results of severe introspection when he speaks of the "balancing of egoistic and altruistic motive in our conduct":

> Often enough altruism is there chiefly in profession or at best a quite superficial will which does not belong to the centre of our action; it becomes then either a deliberate or else a half-conscious camouflage by which egoism masks itself and gets at its object without being suspected. But even a sincere altruism hides within itself the ego, and to be able to discover the amount of it hidden up in our most benevolent or even self-sacrificing actions is the acid test of sincere self-introspection, nor can anyone really quite know himself who has not made ruthlessly this often painful analysis.[48]

---

46 Niebuhr 1986: 130.

47 Niebuhr 2005: 27-28.

48 Aurobindo 1997c: 628.

When we move from the individual to the collective scale, things only become worse. Niebuhr described collective egoism as

> compounded of the egoistic impulses of individuals, which achieve a more vivid expression and a more cumulative effect when they are united in a common impulse than when they express themselves separately.[49]

For Sri Aurobindo, likewise, "a collective egoism, result of the united egoisms of all", was "often an uglier and more barbarous fetish than the egoism of the individual".[50]

Yet these sobering perceptions did not lead Sri Aurobindo to despair about humanity. Nor did Niebuhr's similar unmasking of an all-pervasive egoism cause him to renounce his qualified optimism about our destiny. "An adequate religion," he pointed out, "is always an ultimate optimism which has entertained all the facts which lead to pessimism." Elaborating on the grounds for this optimism, he explained, that it

> is based upon a faith in a transcendent center of meaning which is never fully expressed in any partial value and is never exhausted in any concrete historical reality. But though it is not exhausted in any such reality it is incarnated there.[51]

Niebuhr's ultimate optimism translated into a hope that humankind's divisions, inequalities and mutual misunderstandings can be progressively overcome:

> There are no limits to be set in history for the achievement of more universal brotherhood, for the development of more perfect and more inclusive mutual relations. All the characteristic hopes and aspirations of Renaissance and Enlightenment, of both secular and Christian liberalism are

---

49 Niebuhr 2005: xii.

50 Aurobindo 1998a: 255.

51 Niebuhr 1986: 6.

> right at least in this, that they understand that side of Christian doctrine which regards the *agape* of the Kingdom of God as a resource for infinite developments towards a more perfect brotherhood.[52]

Drawing on his interpretation of Vedanta, Sri Aurobindo foresaw a similar possibility of human unity on a spiritual basis:

> A deeper brotherhood, a yet unfound law of love is the only sure foundation possible for a perfect social evolution, no other can replace it . . . for the Spirit, the inmost self, the universal Godhead in every being is that whose very nature of diverse oneness it is to realise the perfection of its individual life and nature in the existence of all.[53]

America's destiny is inseparable from that of humanity, but has its special potentialities of fulfilment and its own dangers of going astray. Niebuhr saw as assets the "youthful belief in historic possibilities in our American culture" and the "confidence that problems can be solved". But he cautioned that, in the challenging times ahead of us, "the only possibility of success for our nation and our culture . . . lies in our capacity to make sacrifices and to sustain endeavors without complete certainty of success". He believed that "America's moral and spiritual success in relating itself creatively to a world community requires . . . a reorientation of the whole structure of our idealism", coming to terms with "the limits of all human striving" and "the fragmentariness of all human wisdom". Among other things, there must be "a generous appreciation of the valid elements in the practices and institutions of other nations though they deviate from our own", as well as "a disavowal of the pretentious elements in our original dream, and a recognition of the values and virtues which enter into history in unpredictable ways".[54]

---

52 Niebuhr 1996, vol. 2: 85.

53 Aurobindo 1998a: 220.

54 Niebuhr 2008: 135, 145, 133, 79.

As for Sri Aurobindo, he regarded the "sufficiently widespread eagerness and openness of mind to new things" in America as a "considerable advantage". He added a qualification that is perhaps as applicable today as when it was written early in the last century:

> We have to see whether this will be sufficient to open the mind also to deep and true things. The spiritual future of America is not yet decided; it is in the balance. There is a great possibility before her, but it depends on Americans themselves whether she will make good and realise it.[55]

[55] Aurobindo 2006: 388.

7

Intuition and the Limits of Reason

A Cross-Cultural Study

For now we see through a glass, darkly; but then face to face: now I know in part; but then shall I know even as also I am known.
– Paul the Apostle, 1 Corinthians 13.12 (King James version)

Philosophers, in spite of their apparent divergencies, agree in distinguishing two profoundly different ways of knowing a thing. The first implies that we move round the object; the second that we enter into it. . . . The first kind of knowledge may be said to stop at the relative; the second, in those cases where it is possible, to attain the absolute. – Henri Bergson 1912: 1

Vedantic psychology explores the idea and intuition of a higher reality than mind.

The intuition can only be verified by psychological experience exceeding the normal action of mind. This experience may lead to constantly ascending intuitions verified by an ascent of experience to some summit of being. – Sri Aurobindo 1997: 311

Subjective and Objective Knowledge

No activity defines our humanity more than the pursuit of knowledge. This perennial seeking has taken many forms reflecting the cultural and temperamental diversity of humankind. But certain common problems arise from the nature of our consciousness itself. What exactly do we mean by knowledge? Where should we look for it, within ourselves or outside? By what means can we find it? How far is it even attainable? Collectively is our knowledge advancing toward completeness or is it a fragmentary remnant of what was revealed to our ancestors? Over the ages, such questions have elicited sometimes similar, sometimes contrasting responses in different parts of the world.

A recurrent set of questions pertains to the relation of reason to intuition. Which is more reliable, discursive thought or immediate insight? Is one superior to the other or do we need both? Formulated and answered in various ways, these questions regarding our means of cognition are connected to the difference between subjective and objective knowledge. That distinction is imposed by the very structure of our awareness. We have intimate access to our own being, at least in its surface movements. External objects and other beings are presented to us more indirectly through the machinery of sensation.

Accordingly, one view of the proper orientation of the quest for knowledge is represented by the ancient Greek injunction, "Know thyself" (*gnōthi seauton*). But the Greeks were also among the first to systematically investigate the world perceived by the senses. Indeed, Eurocentric historians have traced the antecedents of modern science almost exclusively to the Greeks. They minimize the contributions of the Arabs, Egyptians, Chinese and Indians, whose influences converging in early modern Europe helped to make the Scientific Revolution possible.[1]

Both subjective and objective knowledge have been cultivated in every civilization. Usually, however, there has been an emphasis on one or the other. In India, for example, the Upaniṣads spoke of the knowledge of this world as the lower knowledge (*aparā vidyā*). This included subjects such as astronomy and linguistics, to which ancient India made major contributions. But the knowledge of the universal spirit

---

[1] See Bala 2006.

(*Brahman*), attained through self-realization, was regarded as the higher knowledge (*parā vidyā*), which being known, all is known.[2] At the other end of the spectrum, modern Western culture has tended to reverse this ranking and treat science as the key to understanding everything. Even in psychology, introspection was rejected by behaviorists and has hardly been rehabilitated by cognitive psychologists. If not spirit but matter is that which being known, all is known, the logical conclusion is that mental processes including thought, art and spirituality can be fully explained by analyzing the brain.

Inward-looking and outward-looking approaches to the pursuit of truth need not be mutually exclusive. On the contrary, a synthesis of the results of subjective and objective, intuitive and rational methods ought to offer the most complete and balanced perspective on our existence in this perplexing universe. Even in the "hard" sciences, as we will see, the most decisive advances have sometimes been achieved by a fusion of rigorous mathematical thinking with almost mystical insight.

Plato, Aristotle and Quantum Physics

The origins of two sides of Western thought are often associated with the names of Plato and Aristotle. The stereotypes of these founding fathers of the occidental tradition are summed up in a piece of doggerel suggesting a dichotomy between Aristotle's down-to-earth empiricism and Plato's intoxication with pure Ideas:

Said Aristotle unto Plato,
"Have another sweet potato?"
Said Plato unto Aristotle,
"Thank you, I prefer the bottle."[3]

---

2 *Muṇḍaka Upaniṣad* 1.1.3. See Aurobindo 2001a: 131.

3 Attributed to the American writer Owen Wister (1860–1938). Quoted in Dickson 2009: 179.

On a higher level of culture, the figures of Plato and Aristotle are central to Raphael's monumental fresco *The School of Athens*, painted on a wall of a room in the Vatican between 1509 and 1511. Cultural historian Richard Tarnas comments in *The Passion of the Western Mind*:

> There, in the center of the many Greek philosophers and scientists gathered in lively discussion, stand the elder Plato and the younger Aristotle, with Plato pointing upward to the heavens, to the invisible and transcendent, while Aristotle motions his hand outward and down to the earth, to the visible and immanent.

Thus we find artistically rendered "a certain elegant balance and tension between empirical analysis and spiritual

intuition".[4] This Hellenic balance was recovered in the Renaissance, when it was embodied most splendidly in the many-sided genius of Leonardo da Vinci (on whom Raphael modeled his Plato). In other periods of European culture, the delicate balance has sometimes been preserved less successfully by the Greeks' intellectual descendants.

4 Tarnas 1991: 68.

Raphael's visual characterization of the two great philosophers, though broadly justified, simplifies a complex relationship. Intuition of the transcendent does not account for the whole of Plato's thought, whose analytical side paved the way for Aristotelian logic. Aristotle, for his part, was not quite as earth-bound as his gesture in the painting seems to indicate. He once wrote in the exalted spirit of his teacher:

> We must not listen to those who urge us to think human thoughts since we are human, and mortal thoughts since we are mortal; rather, we should as far as possible immortalize ourselves and do all we can to live by the finest element in us – for if in bulk it is small, in power and worth it is far greater than anything else.[5]

European philosophy was famously described by Whitehead as a series of footnotes to Plato.[6] On the other hand, Western science would appear to be much more indebted to Aristotle, who was a pioneer of the investigation of the natural world and the founder of biology, among other achievements. Yet Plato has been surprisingly influential at certain critical junctures in the history of science. With regard to the Scientific Revolution of the seventeenth century, the physicist Werner Heisenberg noted:

> It is certainly no accident that the beginnings of modern science were associated with a turning away from Aristotle and a reversion to Plato.[7]

This was partly because the official Aristotelianism of Galileo's time was a fossilized orthodoxy that had to be challenged if science was to progress. Aristotle himself can hardly be blamed for the distortion of his legacy by the misguided zeal of his admirers. Galileo, whose lifelong quarrel was with Aristotelian philosophers more than with the Church, remarked:

---

5 Aristotle, *Nicomachean Ethics*, X.7, 1177b-31–5, tr. in Barnes 2000: 3.

6 Whitehead 1978: 39.

7 Wilber 2001: 40.

> I often wonder how it can be that these strict supporters of Aristotle's every word fail to perceive how great a hindrance to his credit and reputation they are, and how the more they desire to increase his authority, the more they actually detract from it.[8]

But there was a more fundamental reason why Plato's role in inspiring the Scientific Revolution – and later, quantum physics – paradoxically overshadows in some ways that of Aristotle, the father of Western science. Aristotelian empiricism, as Heisenberg explained, was prone to accept sensory experience at face value. At a certain point, science had to liberate itself from the kind of experience that tells us, for instance, that the earth is at rest and the sun moves around it, or that the ground beneath our feet is solid. This was replaced "by an idealization of experience, which claims to be recognized as the correct idealization by virtue of the fact that it allows mathematical structures to become visible in the phenomena".[9] This idealization is closer to the spirit of Pythagoras and Plato than to that of Democritus and Aristotle. At the same time, as Heisenberg acknowledged, pure mathematical speculation is as unfruitful as pure empiricism for arriving at a valid representation of natural phenomena. Giving both Aristotle and Plato their due, he concludes:

> Only from the tension, the interplay between the wealth of facts and the mathematical forms that may possibly be appropriate to them, can decisive advances spring.[10]

Heisenberg's role in important advances in quantum physics gives a particular interest to his observations on the process of scientific discovery. Describing such discovery as the "shining forth of the beautiful into exact science", he asks how

---

8 Galilei 2001: 129.

9 Wilber 2001: 41.

10 Ibid.: 61.

it is that "the great connection becomes recognizable, even before it is understood in detail and before it can be rationally demonstrated? In what does the power of illumination consist, and what effect does it have on the onward progress of science?"[11] To answer these questions he draws on Plato.

The "immediate recognition" of what Heisenberg calls "the great connection" is, he maintains, "not a consequence of discursive (i.e., rational) thinking".[12] Rather,

> the apprehension of Ideas [in the Platonic sense] by the human mind is more an artistic intuiting, a half-conscious intimation, than a knowledge conveyed by the understanding. It is a reminiscence of forms that were already implanted in this soul before its existence on earth. . . . Something is evoked in it that was not imparted to it from without by the senses but has always been already laid down there in a deeply unconscious region.[13]

Heisenberg supports this view with a quotation from another pioneer of quantum theory, Wolfgang Pauli, who also refers to Plato:

> The process of understanding in nature, together with the joy that man feels in understanding, i.e., in becoming acquainted with new knowledge, seems therefore to rest upon a correspondence, a coming into congruence of pre-existent internal images of the human psyche with external objects and their behavior. This view of natural knowledge goes back, of course, to Plato and was . . . also very plainly adopted by Kepler. The latter speaks, in fact, of Ideas, preexistent in the mind of God and imprinted accordingly upon the soul, as the image of God. These primal images, which the soul can perceive by means of an innate instinct, Kepler calls archetypes. There is a very wide-ranging

11 Wilber 2001: 63.

12 Ibid.: 65.

13 Ibid.: 59-60.

> agreement here with the primordial images or archetypes introduced into modern psychology by C.G. Jung.[14]

Heisenberg's reminiscence of the breakthroughs in which he participated as a young man in his twenties shows how deeply Plato could still speak to some of the most brilliant and original minds of our age. After Planck's discovery of the quantum properties of light in 1900, a crisis had overtaken physics during the first quarter of the twentieth century as the Newtonian model began to break down. To explain how this crisis was resolved, Heisenberg offers a Platonic account of the phenomenon of understanding. Generalizing what must have been a powerful personal experience, he describes how a protracted period "inaugurated by processes in the unconscious long before the content of consciousness can be rationally formulated" leads to the point where "the true Ideas rise up" in one's awareness:

> At that moment . . . there occurs in the soul of him who sees them an altogether indescribable process of the highest intensity. It is the amazed awe that Plato speaks of in the *Phaedrus*, with which the soul remembers, as it were, something it had unconsciously possessed all along.[15]

Logical Positivism and Truth

"Truth dwells in the deeps", wrote the German poet and philosopher Friedrich Schiller in a line often quoted by Niels Bohr, to whom we largely owe the present model of the structure of the atom. In a conversation with Heisenberg and Pauli, Bohr commented on the logical positivism that has dominated much of modern philosophy:

> For my part, I can readily agree with the positivists about the things they want, but not about the things they reject. . . . Positivist insistence on conceptual clarity is, of course,

14 Wilber 2001: 66-67.

15 Ibid.: 68.

> something I fully endorse, but their prohibition of any discussion of the wider issues, simply because we lack clear-cut enough concepts in this realm, does not seem very useful to me – this same ban would prevent our understanding of quantum theory.[16]

Bohr's reflections led him to formulate a proposition he called "the complementarity between clarity and truth". In Pauli's words, this states that

> if an assertion is too clear, then there is something wrong with its accuracy, and if an assertion is true, then its clarity is limited. For every truth also contains in part something unknown, only glimpsed and therefore also a hidden opposite to its conscious meaning.[17]

Heisenberg, Pauli and Bohr were not the only physicists in the early twentieth century whose philosophical outlooks were incompatible with a narrow positivism. Albert Einstein considered the true scientific search for knowledge to have a religious dimension, inspired by something akin to Spinoza's *amor Dei intellectualis* (intellectual love of God). The thought of the seventeenth-century Dutch philosopher Baruch Spinoza has been characterized as "ecstatic rationalism".[18] It exerted a profound influence on Einstein. Spinoza associates the "intellectual love of God" with intuitive knowledge (*scientia intuitiva*). In his system this is the highest of three levels of cognition, superior to ordinary reasoning. He does not, however, elevate intuition at the expense of reason, but regards it as supremely rational in its nature.

In the spirit of Spinoza, Einstein writes of scientific discovery that "whoever has undergone the intense experience of successful advances made in this domain is moved by

---

16 Wilber 2001: 34.

17 Gieser 2005: 28.

18 Goldstein 2006: 186.

profound reverence for the rationality made manifest in existence". Clarifying his conception of the relationship between science and religion, he continues:

> By way of the understanding he achieves a far-reaching emancipation from the shackles of personal hopes and desires, and thereby attains that humble attitude of mind toward the grandeur of reason incarnate in existence, and which, in its profoundest depths, is inaccessible to man. This attitude, however, appears to me to be religious in the highest sense of the word. And so it seems to me that science not only purifies the religious impulse of the dross of its anthropomorphism, but also contributes to a religious spiritualization of our understanding of life.[19]

Louis de Broglie, whose work led to the development of wave mechanics, reflects like Einstein on the nature of the "mysterious attraction" that leads some to dedicate themselves to science:

> The great epoch-making discoveries in the history of science (think, for example, of that of universal gravitation) have been like sudden lightning flashes, making us perceive in one single glance a harmony up till then unsuspected, and it is to have, from time to time, the divine joy of discovering such harmonies that pure science works without sparing its toil or seeking for profit.[20]

The historian and philosopher of science Thomas Kuhn put forward an influential analysis of these events that alter the course of science. His explanation of how revolutionary science differs from normal science echoes some of the language of de Broglie and other pioneers of scientific discovery:

> Paradigms are not corrigible by normal science at all. Instead . . . normal science ultimately leads only to the recognition

---

[19] Wilber 2001: 113.

[20] Ibid.: 121.

> of anomalies and to crises. And these are terminated, not by deliberation and interpretation, but by a relatively sudden and unstructured event like the gestalt switch. Scientists then often speak of the "scales falling from the eyes" or of the "lightning flash" that "inundates" a previously obscure puzzle, enabling its components to be seen in a new way that for the first time permits its solution. On other occasions the relevant illumination comes in sleep. No ordinary sense of the term "interpretation" fits these flashes of intuition through which a new paradigm is born.[21]

Flashes of intuition are, of course, not restricted to scientists. Nor do all intuitions come in flashes, though the image of lightning piercing the darkness suggests the way a certain kind of intuitive insight is typically experienced. Whereas paradigm shifts occur when the collective practice of normal science has reached a point of crisis, lightninglike intuitions are not confined to such contexts. An intuition may be a private revelation that seems to come out of the blue and is immediately meaningful only to the person who has it.

Ernst Mach, whose philosophy of science was highly influential in the early twentieth century, had such an experience in the 1850s at the age of about seventeen. This is how the forerunner of logical positivism explained the origin of his system of thought:

> On one bright summer day in the open air, the whole world with my ego suddenly appeared to me as a coherent mass of sensations, only more strongly coherent in the ego. Although the actual working-out of this thought did not occur until a later period, yet this moment was decisive for my whole view of the world.[22]

A feature that Mach's epiphany has in common with the revolutionary scientific discoveries described by de Broglie

---

21 Kuhn 1970: 122-23.

22 Moore 1989: 42.

and Kuhn is the comparative suddenness of these events. This characteristic is often attributed to intuition, or at least to some of the psychological phenomena grouped under that heading. The seemingly instantaneous cognition that sees things all at once is called intuition to distinguish it from the slower process of reasoning, as in Mach's later "working-out" of what he saw, or the typical deliberations of Kuhn's "normal science".

The French mathematician Henri Poincaré carefully observed the operation of intuition in his own work. He noticed a pattern. He would begin applying himself to a mathematical problem, but often his initial efforts to solve it produced little or no result. Being brought to a standstill, he would take a rest. But he had evidently "set the unconscious machine in motion". After some time a sudden inspiration would bring the solution. This could happen at any moment; in a case he narrates, it was while he was crossing the street. Or if it occurred after resuming work on the problem, the revelation appeared to be independent of the conscious work, which seemed to serve only as an "unlocking process". This was not the end of it, however; it was still necessary to verify and demonstrate the results. Poincaré summarized his experience in a formula that many mathematicians and scientists would endorse: "it is by logic that we prove, but by intuition that we discover".[23]

Psychologist David Myers mentions a survey of Nobel laureates in science and medicine in which seventy-two out of eighty-three attributed their success partly to intuition. A winner of the prize for medicine said:

> We felt at times there was almost a hand guiding us. We would go from one step to the next, and somehow we would know which was the right way to go, and I really can't tell how we knew that.[24]

---

23 Poincaré 1914: 54-56, 129.

24 Myers 2002: 61.

Turning Eastward

Our study of the nature of intuition and its role in the process of discovery has been confined so far to the European scientific, mathematical and philosophical tradition. The physicist Erwin Schrödinger provides a bridge to the philosophy and spirituality of Asia. Schrödinger was not the only founder of quantum theory who was attracted to the East. Niels Bohr felt an affinity for Taoism, traveled to China and saw parallels between the *yin-yang* concept and the principle of complementarity which he introduced into physics. Werner Heisenberg visited India in the 1930s and acknowledged that his thinking on physics was stimulated by discussions with the Bengali poet Rabindranath Tagore.[25] The East "made a strong impression" on Wolfgang Pauli, who mentioned Vedanta, the I-Ching and Lao Tse as specific philosophical influences.[26] But none of these physicists adopted an Eastern philosophy in the whole-hearted way that Schrödinger did.

Around the age of thirty, Schrödinger became "familiar with Schopenhauer and, through him, with the doctrine of unity taught by the Upanishads". For a while he considered dedicating himself to philosophy rather than science.[27] A few years later, starting from the work of de Broglie, he developed wave mechanics, publishing his findings in 1926 in a rapid series of groundbreaking papers. Schrödinger left no account of how he arrived at the discoveries that, along with the work of a few others including especially Heisenberg, revolutionized physics in the mid-1920s. But it seems unlikely that his Vedantic worldview played no part in his thought process. As his biographer Walter Moore observes, "the unity and continuity of Vedanta are reflected in the unity and continuity of wave mechanics".[28]

---

25 Clarke 1997: 168.

26 Gieser 2005: 27-28.

27 Moore 1989: 109, 111.

28 Ibid.: 173.

Science for Schrödinger was a game where "you strive against the imaginary boundary between yourself and the Godhead – a boundary that perhaps does not exist".[29] Though he revealed few details about how he played this game of scientific discovery, he was more communicative with regard to his spiritual philosophy. Commenting on his favorite phrase in the Upaniṣads – "the words so obscure to the understanding, so close to the intuition: *Tat twam asi*, That Thou Art" – he remarked:

> It is so simple that it is impossible to explain it. It cannot be grasped by the intellect, but it may spring up in you on some occasion like a spark, and then it is there and will never really leave you.[30]

Some millennia ago, the unknown author of the *Kena Upaniṣad* described how such intuitive knowledge can spring up in us:

> This is what it is like: as the lightning flashes and one says "Aha!" or as one blinks and says "Aha!"[31]

Schrödinger elaborated in some of his writings on the view of things that had evidently come to him in such an "Aha!" moment and remained with him from then on. He stressed "the empirical fact that consciousness is never experienced in the plural, only in the singular".[32] This simple fact clinched for him the truth of the Upaniṣadic *tat tvam asi*. That formula expressed the essence of mysticism as Schopenhauer had defined it: "consciousness of the identity of one's own inner being with that of all things".[33] Schrödinger asked:

> What is this Self of yours? What was the necessary condition for making the thing conceived this time into *you*, just *you*,

29 Moore 1989: 348-49.

30 Ibid.: 252, 475.

31 *Kena Upaniṣad* 4.4; my translation.

32 Wilber 2001: 87.

33 Schopenhauer, 1966-69, vol. 2: 613.

> and not someone else? . . . What justifies you in obstinately discovering this difference – the difference between you and someone else – when objectively what is there is *the same*?
>
> Looking and thinking in that manner you may suddenly come to see, in a flash, the profound rightness of the basic conviction in Vedanta: it is not possible that this unity of knowledge, feeling, and choice which you call *your own* should have sprung into being from nothingness at a given moment not so long ago; rather this knowledge, feeling, and choice are essentially eternal and unchangeable and numerically *one* in all men, nay in all sensitive beings.[34]

This is hardly the normal outlook of the Western mind. But the quantum-mechanical world picture itself is as far as possible from common sense. It is not surprising that those who forged this theory were unusual Europeans. Relatively unencumbered by the conventional notions of their own civilization, they were open to radically different ways of seeing things.

The success of the scientific method in unlocking the secrets of the physical universe has given the typical modern mind an unprecedented confidence in the power of reason. This confidence remains largely intact despite the crisis into which civilization has been plunged by the very triumphs of science and its offshoot, technology. Moreover, the new faith in reason is found not only in the West, but everywhere in the world among a Westernized elite. In the wake of European power, the spread of Western rationalism has coincided for some time with the eclipse of cultures where intuitive approaches to knowledge were more highly valued.

Ironically the victories of science, for which the rational intellect usually takes credit, depend on leaps of creative intuition as much as on systematic analysis. The complementary functions of reason and intuition need to be recognized and the dynamics of their interaction explored, without limiting

---

34 Wilber 2001: 97-98. Italics in original.

the scope of the inquiry by Eurocentric preconceptions. If representatives of Asian traditions have something to contribute to our understanding of the workings of intuition, it would be foolish not to listen to them.

The antithesis between the rational, scientific West and the intuitive, mystical East is as much an oversimplification as the supposed opposition between Platonism and Aristotelianism in Western culture itself. Europe's greatest achievements have resulted from the cooperation of Platonic and Aristotelian tendencies. Nevertheless, it is true that the empirical, logical side of the Western pursuit of knowledge has at times overshadowed the more idealistic though no less rational impulse toward transcendence. Sometimes reduced to an undercurrent, it is this Platonic aspect of the Western mind that has the most affinity with corresponding elements in Eastern civilizations.

Some scholars believe that Plato himself was influenced by ideas from India, carried perhaps by Jain missionaries and incorporated in the Orphic Mysteries. Finding support for a speculation to that effect by the French Indologist Alain Daniélou, cultural historian Thomas McEvilley pointed out striking resemblances between Jain teachings and certain Orphic doctrines adopted by Plato.[35] Direct influence may be the simplest explanation of these parallels and would be

35 McEvilley 2002: 197-204. McEvilley writes (pp. 198-99): "The Jains recognized two classes of material particles or atoms: gross particles that make up physical bodies and very fine or small particles that make their way into the soul and stick or cling there. . . . The state of the soul veiled with karmic dirt is likened to that of a wanderer in the world, and the path of wandering is symbolized by a wheel. In Plato's Orphic passages this distinction between two kinds of matter is found, along with the imagery of the dirt, the veil, the wanderer, and the wheel. The matter which makes up the physical body falls away when the body dies; but there is another kind of matter that sticks to the soul in the afterlife and causes it to be reborn."

consistent with what is known about the transmission of ideas in the ancient world.

In modern times, a major Western philosopher on whom Eastern thought made a strong impact was Arthur Schopenhauer. By his own account, his thinking was shaped mainly by Kant, Plato and the Upaniṣads. Despite his pessimistic view of the world, Schopenhauer believed in the possibility of a "better consciousness".[36] His writings reach heights of exaltation in passages where the inspiration of Indian mysticism is felt, as where he evokes the state achieved by the renunciation and extinction of the egoistic will:

> Then, instead of the restless pressure and effort; instead of the constant transition from desire to apprehension and from joy to sorrow; instead of the never-satisfied and never-dying hope that constitutes the life-dream of the man who wills, we see that peace that is higher than all reason, that ocean-like calmness of the spirit, that deep tranquillity, that unshakable confidence and serenity, whose mere reflection in the countenance, as depicted by Raphael and Correggio, is a complete and certain gospel. Only knowledge remains; the will has vanished.[37]

Schopenhauer uses the German equivalent of the word "intuition" in a restricted, Kantian sense. But he describes a kind of perception in which we "let our whole consciousness be filled by the calm contemplation" of the object so that "the person who is involved in this perception is no longer an individual, for in such perception the individual has lost himself; he is *pure*, will-less, painless, timeless *subject of knowledge*".[38]

Schopenhauer's writings were neglected until almost the end of his life, but became immensely popular in cultured

---

36 Janaway 2002: 6, 16-19.

37 Schopenhauer 1966-69, vol. 1: 411.

38 Ibid.: 178-79. Italics in original.

circles in Europe during the half century or so after his death in 1860. They influenced a range of thinkers and creators from Wagner and Nietzsche to Wittgenstein. Few, however, were as open as Schrödinger to the aspects of Schopenhauer's thought that were indebted to the Upaniṣads or converged with Buddhism. Marginalized for most of his career, Schopenhauer was acutely conscious of being out of place in the Europe of his time. He was sympathetic to the fate of Spinoza and Giordano Bruno, commenting wryly:

> They do not belong either to their age or to their part of the globe, which rewarded the one with death, and the other with persecution and ignominy. Their miserable existence and death in this Western world are like that of a tropical plant in Europe. The banks of the Ganges were their spiritual home; there they would have led a peaceful and honoured life among men of like mind.[39]

Epistemologies of Limitation and Epistemologies of Enlightenment

Is a "better consciousness" possible? The sages of the East have always said it is. Plato, Spinoza, Schopenhauer and others in the West have agreed. Plato symbolizes this possibility in his allegory of the cave. We are asked to imagine people chained in a cave who have never seen anything but shadows projected on the wall in front of them. Naturally they take these shadows for reality. Only when one of the captives is freed and emerges into the daylight does he realize how deluded he was.[40]

So it is with us. We now trust science to tell us the nature of things. But as scientists admit, science only analyzes the shadows of Plato's allegory. The early twentieth-century British physicist Sir Arthur Eddington observed:

---

39 Schopenhauer 1966-69, vol. 1: 422, n. 2.

40 Plato, *Republic*, VII, 514-20.

> We have learnt that the exploration of the external world by the methods of physical science leads not to a concrete reality but to a shadow world of symbols, beneath which those methods are unadapted for penetrating.

He added:

> The frank realization that physical science is concerned with a world of shadows is one of the most significant of recent advances.[41]

Eddington's contemporary Sir James Jeans elaborated on this point, referring even more explicitly to Plato's metaphor:

> Many would hold that, from the broad philosophical standpoint, the outstanding achievement of twentieth-century physics is not the theory of relativity with its welding together of space and time, or the theory of quanta with its present apparent negation of the laws of causation, or the dissection of the atom with the resultant discovery that things are not what they seem; it is the general recognition that we are not yet in contact with ultimate reality. We are still imprisoned in our cave, with our backs to the light, and can only watch the shadows on the wall.[42]

Every theory of knowledge must ask whether in the end we can know anything more than shadows. Is our knowledge inherently limited to phenomena, or is it possible to go beyond appearances to the reality that casts the shadow? Depending on their answers, theories of knowledge can be grouped in two categories. Religious scholar Richard King calls them epistemologies of limitation and epistemologies of enlightenment (in the Asiatic sense of "enlightenment").[43] Kant and Śaṅkara may be taken as representative examples from Europe and India. Kant's conclusion was that escaping from

---

41 Wilber 2001: 6-7.

42 Ibid.: 8.

43 King 1999: 182-84.

the cave – to use Plato's image – and perceiving "things in themselves" (*noumena*) is not an option. King points out how Śaṅkara's theory of knowledge has a number of similarities to Kant's, but diverges from it on the fundamental issue of the possibility of unmediated access to reality:

> Śaṅkara's theory of superimposition is reminiscent in some respects of Kant's notion of the "transcendental imagination" – in that we build a picture of reality based upon the manifold of impressions received through the sense-organs which are then structured according to certain concepts that we already possess. . . . For Kant, however, the *a priori* categories constitute the unbreachable conditions of possibility for human experience. These are incontrovertible and binding – as humans we must experience the world according to certain structuring categories such as space and time. Śaṅkara, however, constructs his entire philosophical system based upon the principle that one can transcend the cognitive limitations of current modes of perception and attain the immediacy (*aparokṣatva*) of a direct-cognition of *brahman* (*brahmānubhava*).[44]

Even from Śaṅkara's standpoint, Kant was justified in defining the limits of what reason working on the data supplied by the senses can know. The question is whether these are the limits of all possible knowledge, or whether there is some more direct form of cognition that can lead us out of the cave and its shadows into the sunlight of reality. This is where intuition is often invoked.

In Kantian theories of knowledge, intuition is reduced to being a necessary but inferior faculty associated with sense-perception. Post-Kantian philosophers and psychologists in the West have agreed, with a few notable exceptions, to relegate intuition to a secondary status as an adjunct to our rational consciousness. Its subordinate position is hardly improved by the occasional recognition of its indispensable

---

[44] King 2000: 155.

function and its sometimes remarkable manifestations – as in scientific discovery – which, if admitted, have to be explained by some mechanism of unconscious processing.

Dissenters against the downgrading of intuition have included such figures as Henri Bergson, William James and Alfred North Whitehead; but these distinguished advocates are exceptions to the overall pattern in their fields. Analytic philosophers in the Anglo-American tradition seem particularly fond of intuition bashing.[45] Even since the overthrow of behaviorism by the cognitive revolution, mainstream psychologists remain suspicious of introspection and comparatively uninterested in intuition.[46] The efforts of transpersonalists to elevate its status have had little effect on the general consensus. Of course, the situation in popular culture is very different. But the wave of bestselling books on our intuitive powers only seems to have reinforced the academic aversion for the subject.

Academic anti-intuitivism should be seen in a cross-cultural perspective as well. The assumptions on which it is based are specific to modern Western culture. As King notes, they are not shared by knowledge traditions such as those of India:

> The acceptance of the reality (indeed, for these Indian traditions the *centrality*) of an unmediated and unconstructed awareness constitutes a major point of disagreement between mainstream Western intellectual thought and classical Asian traditions of spirituality. . . . Western epistemologies of limitation reflect the sociocultural and political changes that have occurred in the West since the Enlightenment and thus remain peculiarly Eurocentric in orientation.

Though King himself is far from being an uncritical commentator on Indian philosophy, he goes on to remark pointedly:

---

45 See DePaul and Ramsey 1998: 202.

46 See Hogarth 2001: 6.

> There are other ways of seeing the world than are dreamt of in post-Enlightenment Western philosophy and one should not seek to close one's account on reality too prematurely. To accept modern Western epistemological theories without highlighting their cultural and social particularity is to remain within a long and well-established tradition of Western arrogance about the superiority of Western ways of understanding the world.[47]

Intuition and the Memory of Truth

Eastern philosophies and the disciplines associated with them generally challenge the assumption that our highest capacity is the ability to reason about the world we perceive through our senses. Not that these philosophies are anti-rational. On the contrary, their usual position is that, as Swami Vivekananda put it, "The way to intuition is through reason".[48] Vivekananda distinguished "three grades of manifestation in living beings: (1) subconscious – mechanical, unerring; (2) conscious – knowing, erring; (3) superconscious – intuitional, unerring".[49] When intuition is connected with the superconscious, it can be viewed very differently than it is in systems that recognize only the lower levels.

Sri Aurobindo, who acknowledged Vivekananda's influence, outlined a similar scheme. Accepting the same three levels, he brought out in another way the relation between the first and the third. Vivekananda characterized both of these as "unerring", but associated intuition only with the higher level. Sri Aurobindo attributed intuition to both of them and defined it in a manner that accounts for their differences as well as their similarities:

---

47 King 1999: 182.

48 Vivekananda 1989, vol. 4: 58.

49 Ibid., vol. 8: 17.

> The subconscient and the superconscient are two different formulations of the same All. . . . Intuitional knowledge is that which is common between them and the foundation of intuitional knowledge is conscious or effective identity between that which knows and that which is known. . . . But in the subconscient the intuition manifests itself in the action. . . . In the superconscient . . . the intuition manifests itself in its true nature as knowledge. . . . Between these two states reason and mind act as intermediaries which enable the being to liberate knowledge out of its imprisonment in the act.[50]

The link between the subconscious and the superconscious intuition provides a key to reconciling apparently contradictory viewpoints with regard to this poorly understood faculty.

As an intermediary between the subconscious and the superconscious, reason is the guide that can lead Plato's allegorical prisoners (who are none other than ourselves) to the opening of the cave. Emerging into the light, we will no longer stare at shadowy phenomena, but know things in themselves with a direct vision. Plato's own theory of recollection (*anamnesis*) suggests a modification of the story, however. Perhaps the prisoners have not always been in the cave, but were once free. When they were taken captive, they were hit on the head and lost their memory of the world outside the cave. One of them who then recalls scenes of that other world might experience the "amazed awe" Heisenberg evoked, "with which the soul remembers, as it were, something it had unconsciously possessed all along".[51]

Concurring with Plato, Heisenberg and others, Sri Aurobindo explained intuitive knowledge as "the disclosing

---

50 Aurobindo 2005a: 71-72. The distinction between "reason" and "mind" in the last sentence is the difference between the Sanskrit terms *buddhi* (intellect) and *manas* (sense-mind).

51 Wilber 2001: 68.

of a knowledge that is secret but already existent in the being: it is not an acquisition, but something that was always there and revealable".[52] He applied the Sanskrit word *smṛti* (memory) to this aspect of intuition. *Smṛti* is what occurs

> when the truth is presented to the soul and its truth immediately and directly recognised by a movement resembling memory – a perception that this was always true and already known to the higher consciousness.[53]

An example of this use of the Sanskrit word occurs at the end of the *Bhagavad-Gītā*, where Arjuna says his delusion has been dispelled and he has regained memory (*smṛti*). Elucidating this verse, Sri Aurobindo comments that

> the soul's memory of its self and its truth concealed so long by the misleading shows and forms of our life has returned to it and become its normal consciousness.[54]

Sri Aurobindo was also aware of the Greek antecedents of the explanation of intuition as related to memory. Once, using the Greek name for the goddess of memory, he glossed *smṛti* as "divine mnemosyne", the faculty that "remembers at a second remove the knowledge secret in the being but lost by the mind in the oblivion of the ignorance".[55] Elsewhere he speaks of memory in "that larger sense given to it in Greek thought", where it is not merely "a paltry selection from the store gained by the individual in his present life, but rather the all-recording knowledge which secretly holds and constantly gives from itself everything that we now seem painfully to acquire but really in this sense remember".[56]

---

52 Aurobindo 2005b: 814.

53 Aurobindo 2001a: 430.

54 Aurobindo 1997b: 561.

55 Aurobindo 2001b: 1136.

56 Aurobindo 2005b: 312.

Such ideas, though not alien to Western culture as such, can hardly be said to have received serious attention so far in academic psychology. Transpersonal psychology is an exception. In *Awakening Intuition*, transpersonal psychologist Frances Vaughan writes:

> At any given moment one is conscious of only a small portion of what one knows. Intuition allows one to draw on that vast storehouse of unconscious knowledge that includes not only everything that one has experienced or learned, either consciously or subliminally, but also the infinite reservoir of the collective or universal unconscious, in which individual separateness and ego boundaries are transcended.[57]

The relatively scanty psychological literature on intuition is mostly skeptical of such assertions, if it takes note of them at all. In *Educating Intuition*, Robin Hogarth remarks with reference to Vaughan's book:

> Psychologists working within the scientific tradition would not accept many of Vaughan's statements about intuition.

Nevertheless, Hogarth approves of much of the practical advice that Vaughan offers, including "opening oneself to experience, increasing the ability to observe, and exploring, questioning, and possibly changing one's assumptions about the world". These recommendations are similar to some of his own and can, he feels, "also be advanced from a less mystical point of view".[58]

In *Intuition: Its Powers and Perils*, David Myers tries to "authenticate two huge ideas from contemporary psychological science – that, more than we've realized, *our lives are guided by subterranean intuitive thinking* and that *our intuitions, though speedily efficient, often err in ways we need to understand*. Ergo, intuition – our capacity for direct, immediate knowledge prior

---

57 Vaughan 1979: 4.

58 Hogarth 2001: 281.

to rational analysis – has both surprising potency and surprising perils."[59]

Whatever one's scientific or spiritual standpoint, the emphasis on these perils is not unjustified. Though Vivekananda described the superconscious intuition as unerring, he acknowledged that "in the present state of the world they are few and far between who attain to that state".[60] Sri Aurobindo recognized the limitations and pitfalls of intuition – or pseudo-intuition – and cautioned that

> at the worst, through our misuse of it or false imitations of it, it may lead us into perplexities and confusions which the less ambitious intellectual reason avoids by remaining satisfied with its own safe and plodding method.[61]

Yet the safe plodders do not make the breakthroughs that revolutionize science or change how we look at things. Several of the physicists, philosophers and others whose thought processes we have glimpsed might have substantially agreed with Sri Aurobindo's observations on the relation of intuition to the logical intellect. Reason and intuition, he points out, can very well complement rather than conflict with each other:

> A too formalised logical mind discourages, but a free use of the whole action of the logical intelligence may rather heighten a certain action of immediate insight, the mind's nearest approach to the higher intuition.

The value of the intellect is not in dispute. The question is whether it is enough by itself. Like many others in both the East and the West – including philosophers, mystics and scientists, ancient and modern – Sri Aurobindo did not think so:

> The endeavour of the logical reason is always by a detached, disinterested and carefully founded method to get rid of

---

59 Myers 2002: 128-29. Italics in original.

60 Vivekananda 1989, vol. 4: 59.

61 Aurobindo 2005b: 480.

> error, of prejudgment, of the mind's false confidence and arrive at reliable certitudes.
>
> And if this elaborated method of the mind were really sufficient for truth, there would be no need of any higher step in the evolution of knowledge. . . . It is more and more perceived that the knowledge of phenomena increases, but the knowledge of reality escapes this laborious process. A time must come, is already coming when the mind perceives the necessity of calling to its aid and developing fully the intuition and all the great range of powers that lie concealed behind our vague use of the word and uncertain perception of its significance.[62]

In the past such heightened powers of consciousness were often associated with the revelations that inspired religions and shaped civilizations. Modernity has tended to replace belief in these revelations with faith in reason. But rationalism may be a stage in our preparation for a new and more direct approach to the suprarational, shrouded no longer in a haze of mythology.

For a relatively brief period in recent history, the West forged ahead in the quest for knowledge, as in other areas, while older civilizations retired from the limelight. Those civilizations are now returning to center stage and reinventing themselves under modern conditions. The synergy of intensively interacting cultures cannot fail to stimulate humanity's continuing efforts to understand itself and the universe. Intuition has played an important, if not always acknowledged, role in the advancement of knowledge even in the West at the height of the age of scientific rationalism. All the more are our intuitive faculties likely to flower as Eastern civilizations, which have traditionally cultivated them, assimilate what they have learned from the West, rediscover their own genius and turn their reviving creative energies toward the future.

---

62 Aurobindo 2005b: 854-55.

Bibliography

Aall, Carlo and John Hille, 2010, "Consumption: A Missing Dimension in Climate Policy", in *Interdisciplinarity and Climate Change: Transforming Knowledge and Practice for Our Global Future*, ed. Roy Bhaskar et al., Abingdon, UK: Routledge.

Abou El Fadl, Khaled, 2005, *The Great Theft: Wrestling Islam from the Extremists*, New York: HarperSanFrancisco.

Abu-Lughod, Janet L., 1989, *Before European Hegemony: The World System A.D. 1250–1350*, New York: Oxford University Press.

Albanese, Catherine L., 2007, *A Republic of Mind and Spirit: A Cultural History of American Metaphysical Religion*, New Haven: Yale University Press.

Albrow, Martin, 1996, *The Global Age: State and Society Beyond Modernity*, Stanford, CA: Stanford University Press.

Almond, Gabriel A., R. Scott Appleby and Emmanuel Sivan, 2003, *Strong Religion: The Rise of Fundamentalisms around the World*, Chicago: University of Chicago Press.

Anderson, Benedict, 1991, *Imagined Communities: Reflections on the Origin and Spread of Nationalism*, London: Verso.

Appiah, Kwame Anthony, 2007, *Cosmopolitanism: Ethics in a World of Strangers*, New York: W.W. Norton.

Armstrong, Karen, 2000, *The Battle for God*, New York: Ballantine Books.

Aslan, Reza, 2009, *How to Win a Cosmic War: God, Globalization, and the End of the War on Terror*, New York: Random House.

Aurobindo, Sri, 1993, *Savitri: A Legend and a Symbol*, Pondicherry: Sri Aurobindo Ashram.

———, 1997a, *Essays Divine and Human*, Pondicherry: Sri Aurobindo Ashram.

———, 1997b, *Essays on the Gita*, Pondicherry: Sri Aurobindo Ashram.

———, 1997c, *The Human Cycle, The Ideal of Human Unity, War and Self-Determination*, Pondicherry: Sri Aurobindo Ashram.

———, 1997d, *Karmayogin: Political Writings and Speeches, 1909-1910*, Pondicherry: Sri Aurobindo Ashram.

———, 1998a, *The Human Cycle*, Pondicherry: Sri Aurobindo Ashram.

———, 1998b, *The Ideal of Human Unity*, Pondicherry: Sri Aurobindo Ashram.

———, 1999, *Sri Aurobinder Bangla Rachana*, Pondicherry: Sri Aurobindo Ashram.

———, 2001a, *Kena and Other Upanishads*, Pondicherry: Sri Aurobindo Ashram.

———, 2001b, *Record of Yoga*, Pondicherry: Sri Aurobindo Ashram.

———, 2002, *Bande Mataram: Political Writings and Speeches, 1890–1908*, Pondicherry: Sri Aurobindo Ashram.

———, 2004, *The Renaissance in India and Other Essays on Indian Culture*, Pondicherry: Sri Aurobindo Ashram.

———, 2005a, *The Life Divine*, Pondicherry: Sri Aurobindo Ashram.

———, 2005b, *The Synthesis of Yoga*, Pondicherry: Sri Aurobindo Ashram.

———, 2006, *Autobiographical Notes and Other Writings of Historical Interest*, Pondicherry: Sri Aurobindo Ashram.

———, 2011, *Letters on Himself and the Ashram*, Pondicherry: Sri Aurobindo Ashram.

———, 2012, *The Mother with Letters on the Mother*, Pondicherry: Sri Aurobindo Ashram.

———, 2014, *Letters on Yoga – III*, Pondicherry: Sri Aurobindo Ashram.

Bala, Arun, 2006, *The Dialogue of Civilizations in the Birth of Modern Science*, New York: Palgrave Macmillan.

Barber, Benjamin R., 1996, *Jihad vs. McWorld: How Globalism and Tribalism Are Reshaping the World*, New York: Ballantine.

Banerji, Debashish, 2012, *Seven Quartets of Becoming: A Transformational Yoga Psychology: Based on the Diaries of Sri Aurobindo*, Los Angeles: Nalanda International; New Delhi: D.K. Printworld.

Barnes, Jonathan, 2000, *Aristotle: A Very Short Introduction*, Oxford: Oxford University Press.

Barrows, John Henry, ed., 1893, *The World's Parliament of Religions: An Illustrated and Popular Story of the World's First Parliament of Religions,*

Held in Chicago in Connection with the Columbian Exposition of 1893, Chicago: Parliament Publishing Co.

———, 2007, *The Christian Conquest of Asia*, New Delhi: Logos Press.

Bellitto, Christopher M., Thomas M. Izbicki and Gerald Christianson, eds., 2004, *Introducing Nicholas of Cusa: A Guide to a Renaissance Man*, New York: Paulist Press.

Berger, Peter L., ed., 1999, *The Desecularization of the World: Resurgent Religion and World Politics*, Grand Rapids: William B. Eerdmans.

Berger, Peter L., and Samuel P. Huntington, eds., 2002, *Many Globalizations: Cultural Diversity in the Contemporary World*, Oxford: Oxford University Press.

Bergson, Henri, 1912, *An Introduction to Metaphysics*, tr. T.E. Hulme, New York: Knickerbocker Press.

Berlin, Isaiah, 2005, *Liberty*, ed. Henry Hardy, New York: Oxford University Press.

Bhaskar, Roy, Cheryl Frank, Karl Georg Hoyer, Petter Naess and Jenneth Parker, eds., 2010, *Interdisciplinarity and Climate Change: Transforming Knowledge and Practice for Our Global Future*, Abingdon, UK: Routledge.

Biechler, James, 2004, "Interreligious Dialogue", in *Introducing Nicholas of Cusa: A Guide to a Renaissance Man*, ed. Christopher Bellitto, Thomas Izbicki and Gerald Christianson, New York: Paulist Press.

Bose, Sugata, 2013, "The Spirit and Form of an Ethical Polity: A Meditation on Aurobindo's Thought", in *Situating Sri Aurobindo: A Reader*, ed. Peter Heehs, New Delhi: Oxford University Press.

Boulding, Kenneth E., 1956, *The Image: Knowledge in Life and Society*, Ann Arbor, MI: University of Michigan Press.

Bramen, Carrie Tirado, 2000, *The Uses of Variety: Modern Americanism and the Quest for National Distinctiveness*, Cambridge: Harvard University Press.

Brathwaite, Edward Kamau, 1973, *The Arrivants: A New World Trilogy*, Oxford: Oxford University Press.

Braudel, Fernand, 1993, *A History of Civilizations*, tr. Richard Mayne, New York: Penguin Books.

Burke, Marie Louise, 1992, *Swami Vivekananda in the West: New Discoveries*, Calcutta: Advaita Ashrama.

Bury, J.B., 1955, *The Idea of Progress: An Inquiry into its Origin and Growth*, New York: Dover.

Chan, Wing-tsit, ed., 1969, *A Source Book in Chinese Philosophy*, Princeton, NJ: Princeton University Press.

Chanda, Nayan, 2007, *Bound Together: How Traders, Preachers, Adventurers, and Warriors Shaped Globalization*, New Delhi: Penguin Books.

Chapman, J. Wilbur, 1900, *The Life and Work of Dwight Lyman Moody*, Philadelphia: International Publishing Co. http://www.biblebelievers.com/moody/.

Chittick, William C, 1994, *Imaginal Worlds: Ibn al-'Arabī and the Problem of Religious Diversity*, Albany, NY: State University of New York Press.

Chua, Amy, 2004, *World on Fire: How Exporting Free Market Democracy Breeds Ethnic Hatred and Global Instability*, New York: Anchor Books.

Clarke, J.J., 1997, *Oriental Enlightenment: The Encounter between Asian and Western Thought*, London: Routledge.

Conze, Edward, 1959, *Buddhism: Its Essence and Development*, New York: Harper & Row.

Corbridge, Stuart, and John Harriss, 2000, *Reinventing India: Liberalization, Hindu Nationalism and Popular Democracy*, Cambridge: Polity Press.

Cowen, Tyler, 2002, *Creative Destruction: How Globalization Is Changing the World's Cultures*, Princeton, NJ: Princeton University Press.

Cox, Robert, 2002, "Civilizations and the Twenty-first Century: Some Theoretical Considerations", in *Globalization and Civilizations*, ed. Mehdi Mozaffari, London: Routledge.

Dalrymple, William, 2011, *Nine Lives: In Search of the Sacred in Modern India*, New York: Vintage Departures.

DePaul, Michael R., and William Ramsey, eds., 1998, *Rethinking Intuition: The Psychology of Intuition and Its Role in Philosophical Inquiry*, Lanham, MD: Rowman & Littlefield.

Dickson, Paul, 2009, *Toasts: Over 1,500 of the Best Toasts, Sentiments, Blessings, and Graces*, New York: Bloomsbury.

Dudziak, Mary L., ed., 2003, *September 11 in History: A Watershed Moment?* Durham, NC: Duke University Press.

Eck, Diana L., 2002, *A New Religious America: How a "Christian Country" Has Become the World's Most Religiously Diverse Nation*, New York: HarperSanFrancisco.

Euben, Roxanne L., 1999, *Enemy in the Mirror: Islamic Fundamentalism and the Limits of Modern Rationalism*, Princeton, NJ: Princeton University Press.

Featherstone, Mike, ed., 1990, *Global Culture: Nationalism, Globalization and Modernity*, London: Sage Publications.

Fernández-Armesto, Felipe, 2000, *Columbus and the Conquest of the Impossible*, London: Phoenix Press.

———, 2001, *Civilizations: Culture, Ambition, and the Transformation of Nature*, New York: Free Press.

Frank, Andre Gunder, 1998, *ReORIENT: Global Economy in the Asian Age*, Berkeley: University of California Press.

Frank, Andre Gunder and Barry Gills, eds., 1996, *The World System: Five Hundred Years or Five Thousand?*, London: Routledge.

Freud, Sigmund, 1959, *Group Psychology and the Analysis of the Ego*, tr. James Strachey, New York: Norton.

Fukuyama, Francis, 2006, *The End of History and the Last Man*, New York: Free Press.

Gaddis, John Lewis, 2002, *The Landscape of History: How Historians Map the Past*, Oxford: Oxford University Press.

Galilei, Galileo, 2001, *Dialogue Concerning the Two Chief World Systems*, tr. Stillman Drake, New York: Modern Library.

Germ, Martin, 2007, "Leonardo's *Vitruvian Man*, Renaissance Humanism, and Nicholas of Cusa", *Umeni (Art)*, **55**(2): 102-07.

Ghemawat, Pankaj, 2011, *World 3.0: Global Prosperity and How to Achieve It*, Boston: Harvard Business Review Press.

Giddens, Anthony, 2003, "The Globalizing of Modernity", in Held and McGrew, eds., *The Global Transformations Reader: An Introduction to the Globalization Debate*, 2nd edn., Cambridge: Polity Press.

Gieser, Suzanne, 2005, *The Innermost Kernel: Depth Psychology and Quantum Physics. Wolfgang Pauli's Dialogue with C.G. Jung*, Berlin: Springer.

Goldberg, Philip, 2010, *American Veda: From Emerson and the Beatles to Yoga and Meditation – How Indian Spirituality Changed the West*, New York: Harmony Books.

Goldstein, Rebecca, 2006, *Betraying Spinoza: The Renegade Jew Who Gave Us Modernity*, New York: Shocken Books.

Goody, Jack, 2006, *The Theft of History*, Cambridge: Cambridge University Press.

Guha, Ramachandra, 2007, *India after Gandhi: The History of the World's Largest Democracy*, New York: Harper Perennial.

Gutmann, Amy, ed., 1994, *Multiculturalism: Examining the Politics of Recognition*, Princeton, NJ: Princeton University Press.

Habermas, Jürgen, 1994, "Struggles for Recognition in the Democratic Constitutional State", tr. Shierry Weber Nicholsen, in *Multiculturalism: Examining the Politics of Recognition*, ed. Amy Gutmann, Princeton, NJ: Princeton University Press.

Hanegraaff, Wouter J., 1998, *New Age Religion and Western Culture: Esotericism in the Mirror of Secular Thought*, Albany, NY: State University of New York Press.

Hansen, Thomas Blom, 1999, *The Saffron Wave: Democracy and Hindu Nationalism in Modern India*, Princeton, NJ: Princeton University Press.

Hasan, Mushirul, 1997, *Legacy of a Divided Nation: India's Muslims since Independence*, New Delhi: Oxford University Press.

Haug, Martin, ed. and tr., 1863, *The Aitareya Brahmana of the Rigveda, Containing the Earliest Speculations of the Brahmans on the Meaning of the Sacrificial Prayers, and on the Origin, Performance, and Sense of the Rites of the Vedic Religion*, 2 vols., Bombay: Government Central Book Depot.

Heehs, Peter, 2006, "The Uses of Sri Aurobindo: Mascot, Whipping Boy, or What?", *Postcolonial Studies*, **9**(2): 151-64.

———, ed., 2013, *Situating Sri Aurobindo: A Reader*, New Delhi: Oxford University Press.

Held, David, and Anthony McGrew, eds., 2003, *The Global Transformations Reader: An Introduction to the Globalization Debate*, 2nd edn., Cambridge: Polity Press.

Hick, John, and Paul F. Knitter, eds., 1987, *The Myth of Christian Uniqueness: Toward a Pluralistic Theology of Religions*, Maryknoll, NY: Orbis Books.

Hobson, John M., 2012, *The Eurocentric Conception of World Politics: Western International Theory, 1760–2010*, Cambridge: Cambridge University Press.

Hogarth, Robin M., 2001, *Educating Intuition*, Chicago: University of Chicago Press.

Huntington, Samuel P., 1997, *The Clash of Civilizations and the Remaking of World Order*, New York: Simon and Schuster.

———, 2000, "The Clash of Civilizations?", in *Globalization and the Challenges of a New Century: A Reader*, ed. Patrick O'Meara, Howard D. Mehlinger, and Matthew Krain, Bloomington, IN: Indiana University Press.

Hutchison, William R., 2003, *Religious Pluralism in America: The Contentious History of a Founding Ideal*, New Haven: Yale University Press.

Ignatieff, Michael, 1998, *The Warrior's Honor: Ethnic War and the Modern Conscience*, New York: Henry Holt.

Irvine, William B., 2009, *A Guide to the Good Life: The Ancient Art of Stoic Joy*, New York: Oxford University Press.

Jackson, Carl T., 1981, *The Oriental Religions and American Thought: Nineteenth-Century Explorations*, Westport, CT: Greenwood Press.

Jacques, Martin, 2012, *When China Rules the World: The End of the Western World and the Birth of a New Global Order*, 2nd edn., New York: Penguin Books.

Jaffrelot, Christophe, 1996, *The Hindu Nationalist Movement and Indian Politics, 1925 to the 1990s: Strategies of Identity-Building, Implantation and Mobilisation*, New Delhi: Penguin/Viking.

Janaway, Christopher, 2002, *Schopenhauer: A Very Short Introduction*, Oxford: Oxford University Press.

Juergensmeyer, Mark, 1993, *The New Cold War? Religious Nationalism Confronts the Secular State*, Berkeley: University of California Press.

Kepel, Gilles, 1994, *The Revenge of God: The Resurgence of Islam, Christianity and Judaism in the Modern World*, tr. Alan Braley, Cambridge: Polity Press.

Khilnani, Sunil, 1998, *The Idea of India*, New Delhi: Penguin Books.

———, 2007, "Nehru's Faith", in *The Crisis of Secularism in India*, ed. Anuradha Needham and Rajeswari Rajan, Durham, NC: Duke University Press.

King, Richard, 1999, *Orientalism and Religion: Postcolonial Theory, India and 'The Mystic East'*, London: Routledge.

———, 2000, *Indian Philosophy: An Introduction to Hindu and Buddhist Thought*, New Delhi: Maya Publishers.

Kolstø, Pål, 2007, "The 'Narcissism of Minor Differences' – Theory: Can It Explain Genocide and Ethnic Conflict?", *Philosophy and Society*, **33**(2): 153-73.

Kuhn, Thomas S., 1970, *The Structure of Scientific Revolutions*, 2nd edn., Chicago: University of Chicago Press.

Kupchan, Charles A., 2012, *No One's World: The West, the Rising Rest, and the Coming Global Turn*, New York: Oxford University Press.

Kymlicka, Will, 2007, *Multicultural Odysseys: Navigating the New International Politics of Diversity*, New York: Oxford University Press.

Leonard, George J., 1994, *Into the Light of Things: The Art of the Commonplace from Wordsworth to John Cage*, Chicago: University of Chicago Press.

Lincoln, Bruce, 2003, *Holy Terrors: Thinking about Religion after September 11*, Chicago: University of Chicago Press.

Lovin, Robin, 2004, "Moral Man and Immoral Society: Rediscovering Reinhold Niebuhr", interview by Krista Tippett, *Speaking of Faith*, 14 December 2004, accessed on 21 April 2014, http://www.onbeing.org/program/moral-man-and-immoral-society-rediscovering-reinhold-niebuhr/extra/complete-transcript-1.

———, 2007, *Reinhold Niebuhr*, Nashville, TN: Abingdon Press.

Mahbubani, Kishore, 2008, *The New Asian Hemisphere: The Irresistible Shift of Global Power to the East*, New York: Public Affairs.

———, 2013, *The Great Convergence: Asia, the West, and the Logic of One World*, New York: Public Affairs.

Malik, Kenan, 2009, *From Fatwa to Jihad: The Rushdie Affair and Its Legacy*, London: Atlantic Books.

Marty, Martin E., 1997, *Modern American Religion*, Volume 1: *The Irony of It All, 1893-1919*, Chicago: University of Chicago Press.

McEvilley, Thomas, 2002, *The Shape of Ancient Thought: Comparative Studies in Greek and Indian Philosophies*, New York: Allworth Press.

McNeill, William H., 1991, *The Rise of the West: A History of the Human Community; with a Retrospective Essay*, Chicago: University of Chicago Press.

Meredith, Robyn, 2007, *The Elephant and the Dragon: The Rise of India and China, and What it Means for All of Us*, New York: W.W. Norton.

Mishra, Pankaj, 2012, *From the Ruins of Empire: The Intellectuals Who Remade Asia*, New York: Farrar, Straus and Giroux.

Montefiore, Simon Sebag, 2005, *Speeches That Changed the World: The Stories and Transcripts of the Moments That Made History*, London: Quercus Publishing.

Moore, Walter, 1989, *Schrödinger: Life and Thought*, Cambridge: Cambridge University Press.

Mother, The, 2004, *Words of the Mother-I*, Pondicherry: Sri Aurobindo Ashram.

Mozaffari, Mehdi, ed., 2002, *Globalization and Civilizations*, London: Routledge.

Myers, David G., 2002, *Intuition: Its Powers and Perils*, New Haven: Yale University Press.

Nederveen Pieterse, Jan, 2009, *Globalization and Culture: Global Mélange*, 2nd edn., Lanham, MD: Rowman and Littlefield.

Needham, Anuradha Dingwaney, and Rajeswari Sunder Rajan, eds., 2007, *The Crisis of Secularism in India*, Durham, NC: Duke University Press.

Nehru, Jawaharlal, 1962, *An Autobiography: With Musings on Recent Events in India*, New Delhi: Allied Publishers.

———, 2010, *The Discovery of India*, New Delhi: Penguin Books.

Ngũgĩ wa Thiong'o, 2009, *Something Torn and New: An African Renaissance*, New York: Basic Civitas Books.

Niebuhr, Reinhold, 1986, *The Essential Reinhold Niebuhr: Selected Essays and Addresses*, ed. Robert McAfee Brown, New Haven: Yale University Press.

———, 1996, *The Nature and Destiny of Man: A Christian Interpretation*, 2 vols., Louisville, KY: Westminster John Knox Press.

———, 2005, *Moral Man and Immoral Society: A Study in Ethics and Politics*, London: Continuum.

———, 2008, *The Irony of American History*, Chicago: University of Chicago Press.

Nikhilananda, Swami, 1964, *Vivekananda: A Biography*, Calcutta: Advaita Ashrama.

Nirodbaran, ed., 2001, *Talks with Sri Aurobindo*, 2 vols., Pondicherry: Sri Aurobindo Ashram.

Nordau, Max, 1968, *Degeneration*, 1892, repr., New York: Fertig.

Nuo, You, 2009, "In an Unending Search for Spirituality", *China Daily*, 17 December 2009, accessed on 21 April 2014, http://www.chinadaily.com.cn/opinion/2009-12/17/content_9192712.htm.

Nussbaum, Martha C., 2007, *The Clash Within: Democracy, Religious Violence, and India's Future*, Cambridge: Harvard University Press.

O'Meara, Patrick, Howard D. Mehlinger, and Matthew Krain, eds., 2000, *Globalization and the Challenges of a New Century: A Reader*, Bloomington, IN: Indiana University Press.

Overmyer, Daniel L., 1998, *Religions of China: The World as a Living System*, Long Grove, IL: Waveland Press.

Parekh, Bhikhu, 2008, *European Liberalism and 'the Muslim Question'*, Amsterdam: Amsterdam University Press.

Pascal, Blaise, 2005, *Pensées*, tr. Roger Ariew, Indianapolis, IN: Hacket.

Peters, Edward, 1989, *Inquisition*, Berkeley: University of California Press.

Phillips, Anne, 2007, *Multiculturalism without Culture*, Princeton, NJ: Princeton University Press.

Pleyers, Geoffrey, 2010, *Alter-Globalization: Becoming Actors in the Global Age*, Cambridge: Polity Press.

Poincaré, Henri, 1914, *Science and Method*, tr. Francis Maitland, London: Thomas Nelson & Sons.

Prestowitz, Clyde, 2005, *Three Billion New Capitalists: The Great Shift of Wealth and Power to the East*, New York: Basic Books.

Prigogine, Ilya, and Isabelle Stengers, 1985, *Order out of Chaos: Man's New Dialogue with Nature*, London: Flamingo.

Purani, A.B., ed., 2007, *Evening Talks with Sri Aurobindo*, Pondicherry: Sri Aurobindo Ashram.

Race, Alan, 1983, *Christians and Religious Pluralism: Patterns in the Christian Theology of Religions*, Maryknoll, NY: Orbis Books.

Radice, William, ed., 1998, *Swami Vivekananda and the Modernization of Hinduism*, New Delhi: Oxford University Press.

Ramsbotham, Oliver, 2010, *Transforming Violent Conflict: Radical Disagreement, Dialogue and Survival*, London: Routledge.

Rattansi, Ali, 2011, *Multiculturalism: A Very Short Introduction*, New York: Oxford University Press.

Rice, Daniel F., 1993, *Reinhold Niebuhr and John Dewey: An American Odyssey*, Albany, NY: State University of New York.

Robertson, Roland, 1992, *Globalization: Social Theory and Global Culture*, London: Sage.

Rolland, Romain, 2004, *The Life of Vivekananda and the Universal Gospel: A Study of Mysticism and Action in Living India*, tr. E.F. Malcolm-Smith, Kolkata: Advaita Ashrama.

Rubenstein, Richard E., 1999, *When Jesus Became God: The Struggle to Define Christianity during the Last Days of Rome*, Orlando, FL: Harcourt.

Sachs, Wolfgang, ed., 1993, *Global Ecology: A New Arena of Political Conflict*, London: Zed Books.

Sacks, Jonathan, 2002, *The Dignity of Difference: How to Avoid the Clash of Civilizations*, London: Continuum Press.

Sagan, Carl, 1997, *Pale Blue Dot: A Vision of the Human Future in Space*, New York: Ballantine Books.

Samartha, Stanley, 1987, "The Cross and the Rainbow: Christ in a Multireligious Culture", in *The Myth of Christian Uniqueness: Toward a Pluralistic Theology of Religions*, ed. John Hick and Paul Knitter, Maryknoll, NY: Orbis Books.

Sangharakshita, Bhikshu, 1983, *Anagarika Dharmapala: A Biographical Sketch*, Kandy: Buddhist Publication Society.

Schmidt, Leigh Eric, 2005, *Restless Souls: The Making of American Spirituality*, New York: HarperSanFrancisco.

Schopenhauer, Arthur, 1966-69, *The World as Will and Representation*, tr. E.F.J. Payne, 2 vols., New York: Dover.

Seager, Richard Hughes, 1995, *The World's Parliament of Religions: The East/West Encounter, Chicago, 1893*, Bloomington, IN: Indiana University Press.

Seager, Richard Hughes, and Ronald R. Kidd, eds., 1993, *The Dawn of Religious Pluralism: Voices from the World's Parliament of Religions, 1893*, La Salle, IL: Open Court.

Sen, Amartya, 1997, *Human Rights and Asian Value*, New York: Carnegie Council on Ethics and International Affairs.

———, 2006, *Identity and Violence: The Illusion of Destiny*, London: Allen Lane.

Sen, Amiya P., 2000, *Swami Vivekananda*, New Delhi: Oxford University Press.

Sengupta, Sukalyan, and Makarand Paranjape, eds., 2005, *The Cyclonic Swami: Vivekananda in the West*, New Delhi: Samvad India Foundation.

Shapiro, Fred, 2008, "Who wrote the Serenity Prayer", *Yale Alumni Magazine*, vol. 71, no. 6, accessed on 21 April 2014, http://archives.yalealumnimagazine.com/issues/2008_07/serenity.html.

Sharma, Jyotirmaya, 2003, *Hindutva: Exploring the Idea of Hindu Nationalism*, New Delhi: Penguin/Viking.

Sifton, Elisabeth, 2005, *The Serenity Prayer: Faith and Politics in Times of Peace and War*, New York: W.W. Norton & Company.

Soguk, Nevzat, 2011, *Globalization and Islamism: Beyond Fundamentalism*, Lanham, MD: Rowman & Littlefield.

Stannard, David E., 1992, *American Holocaust: The Conquest of the New World*, New York: Oxford University Press.

Steger, Manfred B., 2003, *Globalization: A Very Short Introduction*, New York: Oxford University Press.

———, 2009, *Globalisms: The Great Ideological Struggle of the Twenty-First Century*, Lanham, MD: Rowman & Littlefield.

Strong, Josiah, 1893, *The New Era: Or, The Coming Kingdom*, New York: Baker & Taylor.

Tarnas, Richard, 1991, *The Passion of the Western Mind: Understanding the Ideas That Have Shaped Our World View*, New York: Ballantine Books.

Taylor, Charles, 1994, "The Politics of Recognition", in Gutmann, *Multiculturalism: Examining the Politics of Recognition*, Princeton, NJ: Princeton University Press.

Tharoor, Shashi, 2012, *Nehru: The Invention of India*, New Delhi: Penguin Books.

———, 2013, *Pax Indica: India and the World of the Twenty-first Century*, New Delhi: Penguin Books.

Toynbee, Arnold, 1953, *The World and the West*, London: Oxford University Press.

Vaughan, Frances E., 1979, *Awakening Intuition*, New York: Doubleday.

Vivekananda, Swami, 1989, *The Complete Works of Swami Vivekananda*, 8 vols., Calcutta: Advaita Ashrama.

Wallerstein, Immanuel, 2004, *World-Systems Analysis: An Introduction*, Durham, NC: Duke University Press.

Wernick, Andrew, 2005, *Auguste Comte and the Religion of Humanity: The Post-Theistic Program of French Social Theory*, Cambridge: Cambridge University Press.

Whitehead, Alfred North, 1978, *Process and Reality*, New York: Free Press.

Wilber, Ken, ed., 2001, *Quantum Questions: Mystical Writings of the World's Great Physicists*, Boston: Shambhala.

Wills, Gary, 2007, *Head and Heart: American Christianities*, New York: Penguin.

Wriggins, Salley Hovey, 2004, *The Silk Road Journey with Xuanzang*, Boulder, CO: Westview Press.

Yao, Xinzhong, 2000, *An Introduction to Confucianism*, Cambridge: Cambridge University Press.

Zakaria, Fareed, 2012, *The Post-American World: Release 2.0*, New York: W.W. Norton.

Index